THE DAY JOB

TERRY WOGAN

THE DAY JOB

illustrations by Hector Breeze

A Futura Book
Macdonald Futura Publishers

A Futura Book

First published in 1981 by
Queen Anne Press
Macdonald Futura Publishers Limited

First Futura edition 1982

Copyright © Terry Wogan 1981

ISBN 0 7088 2208 8

Produced by Lennard Books,
The Old School,
Wheathampstead, Herts AL4 8AN

Editor Michael Leitch
Designed by David Pocknell's Company Limited
Production Reynolds Clark Associates Limited
Printed and bound in Yugoslavia by
Mladinska Knjiga, Ljubljana

The author and publishers are grateful to the owners of
copyright material for kindly granting permission for its
use in the book. Every effort has been made to trace the
authors of contributions included, and thanks and
apologies are extended to anyone who for any reason may
not have been contacted.
Back cover contributed by Barry Dugdale, Sunderland.

Photograph on page 70
by W T Ellary.
Published by courtesy of the
Express Lift Company Limited

Futura Publications
A division of Macdonald & Co (Publishers) Ltd
Maxwell House
74 Worship Street
London
EC2A 2EN

Contents

Preface

There's not a bit of use diving for cover behind the chaise-longue, Hermione, he's got another one out. Another sickening dig to the soft underbelly of The Great British Book-Buying Public. Another nail in the coffin of the world's greatest literary tradition. What in Heaven's name possesses them to encourage the bounder? It's not as if his first effort went well – I know for a fact that he's got 20,000 unsold copies of the thing in his garage. Not surprising when you remember some of the reviews:

– 'Damned thing doesn't even have an index' *(Times Literary Supplement)*

– 'Anthony Burgess need not fret' *(The Listener)*

– 'I think I'm going to be sick' (Bernard Levin)

Picture if you can the bemused expression of *this* unfortunate, who obviously won it as a booby-prize in the York Sea Scouts' Annual Tombola:

Dear Terry,

Re: Your 'Book'

With great justification, your listeners fire tirades of abuse and a barrage of contumely over your flaccid, lacklustre performances on radio and TV.

However, your new book is a different story – it does for the literary movement all that Eddie Waring has done for the Royal Ballet.

Ralph Magee,
York.

It's not as if he's even *liked!* What about all those halfpennies, gathered by toddlers and discerning listeners alike, for the Send Terry Wogan To Patagonia Fund? The swine then put them in the poor-box for Sick and Indigent Radio Producers and wouldn't go! Some cock-and-bull excuse about Patagonia being full of Welshmen and shrinking from the prospect of a Max Boyce with maraccas....

He's shredding the very fabric of British Society, I tell you – cocking a deviated septum at All That's Best In Our Society. Why, the rotter is even sundering our more happily married couples. Take a gander at this:

Mr Wogan,
You are a nuisance. I am nearing the end of my two weeks holiday during which I was hoping to have a complete rest and lay in bed in the mornings. Little did I know that my wife is a fan of yours and insists on listening to your waffle every morning. Please note that since I have to book my holidays in February I shall require notice from you in January as to when you will be off so that I can take the same days. Failure to comply will result in my writing you a nasty letter.

Dear Terry,
Ignore the above ramblings as my beloved husband really enjoys your programme and wishes it lasted longer. I must admit your cheery chatter acts like a tonic and starts my day off right. Margaret.

I always suspected she was a bit simple, (resumed the husband) *and if ever you come over the border like that Hamilton fellow did recently, then I'll set my pet fishcake on to you.*

*E. R. Gammon,
Brechin, Angus.*

Proof, if proof were needed. I ask you, is this the kind of book you'd want to leave lying around for the children and servants to read?

It's a funny business

Since you didn't ask, I was born in Limerick, with catarrh. This is no slur on that somewhat moist gem set in the verdant delta of the Shannon. There are worse things than catarrh, though not in the early morning, if you happen to be married to a sufferer. Look at Jimmy Young, if you can bear it, and he was born in Gloucestershire! I live in the Thames Valley now, and that makes my catarrh worse, so you can't entirely blame Limerick. I blame my nose, it seems to have an unerring instinct for humidity. The unfortunate proboscis is probably only getting its own back, anyway, for the appalling treatment it received during my youth. I know what you're thinking, and it's not *that* – I was a delicately nurtured youth, with short finger-nails and impeccably starched handkerchiefs. But, I was a rugby player in my youth and early manhood – ah the manly camaraderie of the showers – and on the field the old hooter, although Heaven knows, hardly in the Cyrano de Bergerac class, was ever the brunt of some hairy agricultural eejit, who would persist in taking the short cut through me, rather than around, and for some reason the old nose was always the first to go. We used to wear shin-guards and gum-shields, but nothing for the nasal extremity. Something like a Norman soldier's helmet might have been a good idea....

Nose apart, the rest of me had a fairly uneventful childhood in Limerick, apart from the rain. The few sepia prints extant show me as a somewhat chubby (hard to believe, isn't it?) little fellow, with short trousers just a shade too long, but generously masking an unwholesome pair of knees.

Most of my memories of childhood are of the resonant baritone of my father reverberating from the bathroom. He used to sing while he was shaving, and a bloody business it was, too. Sometimes our bathroom resembled nothing so much as Sweeney Todd's on a Saturday night. My father's well-worn favourites were Victorian crowd-pleasers such as 'Many Brave Hearts Lie Asleep In The Deep', or 'Dead for Bread'. He favoured the more bravura baritone arias from opera, such as 'Valentine's Goodbye' from 'Faust', and it can only have been a merciful providence that spared us *Lieder*.

I remember, too, the Sundays we would go fishing together – or, rather, we should arrive at river or shore, and get *ready* to fish. A meticulous man, he would spend hours tying flies, and talking of days spent tickling trout in Wicklow mountain streams, and then, with the sun going down and the last of the sandwiches an indigestible memory, we would head

FOR HEAVEN'S
SAKE, DAD –
GROW A
BEARD !

for home.... Ever since, I've been unable to prepare properly for anything (as any regular listener, etc).

At school, although I occasionally took part in debates, and trod the boards in the statutory D'Oyly Carte extravaganzas, I was far from being the life and soul of the classroom. 'Shy and introverted' would describe me better, and I find it extraordinary how many people in the theatre, television and radio also fit that description. Here we have a medium that is tailor-made for the extrovert, the gregarious show-off, and it's chock-full of people who are struck mumchance if they can't hide behind a role, a microphone or a camera. Introverted egotists, that's what we are, and yes, we like to be thought of as 'shy.' Shy's nice – it bespeaks an engaging modesty, a lack of bombast and self-importance. Now that I think of it, you won't hear too many people in show-business admitting to being show-offs.

When I was 15, Limerick having had its fill of Wogans, we left in a masked manner for the teeming metropolis of Dublin, a city whose main claim to fame at the time was the length of its cinema queues and the splendour of its ice-cream parlours; at least, as far as one 'culchie' was concerned. (A native of Dublin is a 'gurrier'; anyone unfortunate enough to be born on the wrong side of the Dublin mountains is a 'bogman,' a 'culchie,' probably lured from his hovel by the promise of raw meat.) Heaven, in the Dublin of those days, was a seat in the stalls and a Knickerbocker Glory afterwards.

I suppose the reason I'm not really 'show-biz' is because I missed the great days of variety and the clamour of the music-hall. I'm a child of the radio-cinema generation. My sense of humour, my view of life were coloured, enhanced and ultimately influenced by the great radio shows of the '50s: 'Hancock's Half-Hour,' 'Take It From Here,' 'The Goon Show.' The Light Programme was my life-line and I listened with an avidity unmatched by any of my school-mates. So, I can't really be too hard on my children when they seem transfixed by the old goggle-box; all I can hope is that it has the same benign influence on them that radio had on me.

Like all my contemporaries, I loved the cinema, particularly musicals. Probably, I was a little young for the sophisticated Astaire and Rogers, for my affections lay more with Doris Day and Donald O'Connor. One of Dublin's features, apart from the aforementioned queues, was 'Cine-Variety.' At least three large cinema-theatres in the city would stage marathon combinations of variety and film shows, the largest and the best being the Theatre Royal. Their show included an organist, pit orchestra, dancing girls, speciality act, comedian followed by 'B' feature, cartoon, and the 'big' film.

The organist would come rising from the pit, his mighty Wurlitzer ablaze, the words of 'Keep Your Sunny Side Up' flashed on to the screen, complete with bouncing ball, inviting the audience to join in and sing lustily. In all the years I went to the Theatre Royal, Dublin I never heard a peep out of them. That poor organist must have had feelings of tempered steel.... That selfsame audience had a short way with comedians as well, which probably explains my own reluctance to 'get out there and kill 'em!' My impressionable youth was masked by the sight of fresh-faced young types trying to do just that, only to be left for dead themselves by waves of indifference from an audience that was only waiting for the movie anyway.

After a course in general philosophy – which seemed to consist mainly in trying to prove my own existence by reason alone – the consensus was that Descartes' reputation had little to fear from my lumbering logic, and that I might be as well off eschewing the intellectual life, and settling for a bit of the old mammon. So I joined the Royal Bank of Ireland. I didn't know what to expect, since I had only been inside a bank a couple of times in my young life, and certainly I'd never thought of it as a career. Looking back, the five years I spent toiling in the service of other people's money seem like a dream. At the time, being a bank clerk was no small thing for a decent Irish lad. You didn't get paid, of course, but you could guarantee other people's passport photographs, and you met a very nice class of girl at the bank socials.

The memories of my years in the financial field are all happy ones. Nay, hysterical. I was fortunate enough to be posted to the Cattle Market branch ('an enviable billet', as the man who taught me how to count notes with my left hand, in the Training School, put it). On all sides, merry cattle jobbers and farmers hurled invective, which mingled easily with the flying sponges of the tellers and the girlish giggles of typists being groped in the safe.

The whole place resembled nothing so much as the Dreamland Ballroom, Muff, on St Patrick's Night, with a bar extension. The manager of the Cattle Market branch of the Royal Bank of Ireland fancied himself a bit of a martinet, and at his worst he did have some of the elusive charm one associates with Attila the Hun. The effect, as Perelman might have put it, was somewhat vitiated by his clothes, which were apparently carved from some left-over gunny sacking, and his footwear, which was invariably children's open-toed sandals.

Still, he was no fool, and I was quickly put to the work best-suited to my talents: sorting two-bob bits from half-crowns, sealing up used notes and carrying them to Head Office. 'Good man, Wogan', the manager would croak at a particularly shrewdly-placed seal. 'There's a future for you in the bank! Neat work. A job well done. The only difference between the difficult and the impossible is that the latter takes a little longer to do, ha-ha! There's no business like show-business, and there's no people like show-people. They laugh when other people cry'.

This view of hard-nosed show-people chuckling away at other people's grief is one I shall carry to the grave. Notes sealed and placed in sturdy leather holdall, I'd set off for Head Office, with the porter as an unwilling bodyguard. We had no means of self-defence, even if we had *wanted* to fight for £5,000 in old notes that smelt strongly of manure, and we took public transport. I like to think the reason we were never attacked was that *nobody* would credit such foolishness – they probably took us for decoys. Sitting ducks we certainly were.

Then, the Bank's Note Department having exchanged our grubby old notes for crisp new ones, the porter and myself would carry the £5,000 round the corner to Bewley's Oriental Cafe to fortify ourselves with bowls of coffee so strong that you felt as if everyone of your nerve-ends was waving away in the breeze. . . .

A job as desirable as that of a bank clerk naturally carried with it heavy social obligations: prospective wives had to be vetted by one's manager, to see if they were acceptable to the bank. The manager was at all times to be addressed as 'Manager' except, of course, in the unlikely event of a social meeting, when he was to be known as 'Mr ——'. Honesty, decency and clean-living were prerequisites as was wearing a tie – but not a blazer, except on Saturday, when it was Liberty Hall. Other members of the staff were to be addressed as 'Mr ——' or 'Miss ——' at all times during office hours, loud laughter was out, singing was a non-starter, and whistling, particularly with your hands in your pockets, was out of the question. All cash shortages had to be made up before the bank closed.

Despite all this, the general ambience of the place was, as I've said, reminiscent of the Moulin Rouge in the paling days of Toulouse-Lautrec: you could not engage in airy badinage with a female customer without being goosed with a broom-handle by a cheery fellow-teller or hit in the eye with a wet sponge. At regular intervals, tellers would sneak into each other's cubicles and tear bank-notes to shreds. Work was to be avoided at all costs, and some unfortunate customer entering the bank with a large lodgment would, like as not, find the place deserted as the tellers, cashiers, accountant and clerk ducked beneath the counter. Some people stood around looking bemused for ten minutes before the manager, alerted by the unearthly hush, restored normal banking services. He himself could often be found locked in the lavatory, which he used as a safe haven, or bunker, to avoid the more aggressive or drunken of his customers.

While in the Bank, perhaps out of frustration, I joined an amateur musical and dramatic society, and enjoyed many hours of innocent fun, slapping on the old 5 and 9, and treading the boards in such well-worn favourites as 'Bitter Sweet', 'Naughty Marietta' and the usual Gilbert and Sullivan gamut. I also used to appear as a 'super', or extra, with the Dublin Grand Opera. I was a Venetian Doge in 'Othello', a waiter in 'La Traviata', a priest in 'Cavalleria Rusticana' and an Ethiopian slave in 'Aida'. An extremely consumptive-looking Ethiopian I must have made too, as I refused to smear the filthy body make-up all over me. I made a slightly anachronistic waiter in 'La Traviata' as well, appearing in suede shoes to the dumb shrieks of the Italian producer. Another night the self-same producer found me drinking in the Green Room of the theatre, when I should have been on-stage in the Easter Procession that is the centre-piece of 'Cavalleria Rusticana'. This severed what might have been a fruitful link between Italian opera and me. 'Aha!' he fumed, catching me in mid-swallow. 'You like to drink your beer? Drink it! The procession show is over! You can go, at home!' I've always been able to take a hint.

One fine day, when I'd been slaving away in the service of mammon for about five years, I answered an ad in an Irish national daily newspaper for an 'announcer/newsreader' required by RTE, the Irish radio and television service, and within three months my whole life had changed.

To my astonishment, I was called for an audition, which I attended having fabricated some tale about a dental appointment, then given a training course, and an offer of part-time employment as an announcer. So, for a short period, I would finish my work in the bank and then dash to RTE in time to read the evening Cattle Market, Stock Market and Weather Reports. Eventually, I was offered a permanent job as an announcer, and without so much as a backward glance I left my permanent, pensionable and eminently respectable position with the bank for the garish glitter-and-tinsel gaiety of the life of the hobbledehoy. There was a lot of head-shaking and tongue-clicking among my elders and betters, of course. There still is, whenever I call in to see them at my old bank; mixed with looks that bespeak a mixture of regret and puzzlement at the foolishness of a quite promising young man, who could possibly have made manager by the time he was 50, but who blew it all away, like a moth to the flame....

I spent eight years with RTE, five of them as a staff announcer, newsreader and presenter, and the rest as a freelance broadcaster. They were happy, exciting years, and whatever success I've achieved in Britain on television and radio is owed, in large part, to the experience I gained in Ireland. I was there for the opening night of Irish television, when, on a wing and a prayer, the new service was launched with an ambitious live outside broadcast. It was snowing, and as a tenor sang with the Army Band for our delight, the passing pedestrians, with that total lack of a sense of occasion that characterizes the Irish, hurled snowballs at the unfortunate singer. It isn't that easy to intone 'Galway Bay' with the precise degree of reverence required when you're ducking, bobbing and weaving in a blizzard.

I behaved with all the usual coltishness of the boy broadcaster in those days: unbuttoning lady-announcers' blouses as they read the news, setting fire to other announcers' scripts, pouring water over people's heads as they broadcast long announcements. One afternoon as I started the half-hour one o'clock news bulletin, my nose began to bleed. Have you any idea how difficult it is to be fair, balanced and well modulated when you're in a blind panic, bleeding to death? Have you any idea how difficult it is to read at all, when the words of the script are being blotted out by huge blobs of your own blood! Let's just say that the Great British Listening Public might have been spared a great deal of heartbreak every morning, if I wasn't such a quick little coagulator....

IT'S THAT WOGAN

In my time on RTE I introduced ceili bands, symphony orchestras, string quartets and pop groups. I read the news, presented record shows, introduced quiz shows and documentaries, and commentated on State Occasions such as President Kennedy's visit, the funeral of an Irish President, and the 50th anniversary of the Easter Rising in Dublin. My commentary position for this last was opposite the Reviewing Stand at the GPO. It was my task to describe the passing parade of pomp and circumstance, and identify the dignitaries on the stand. The parade went by in the manner of all military shows of strength, with the full might of the Irish Navy, Army and Air Force. It didn't take long, so I turned to the Reviewing Stand. With saliva-drying hórror, I realized that I didn't recognize a single distinguished face. No wonder, either, the genius in charge had forgotten to send out the invitations, and at the last minute they had filled up the Reviewing Stand with tourists and onlookers. At times like that a body could wish he had taken the advice of his elders and betters, and stayed in the bank!

I remember introducing guitarists 'live' for television, who promptly fell off their own stools; inviting a quiz-show winner to take a prize, only for her to point out that there weren't any – the production assistant had forgotten them; heart- stopping moments, moments when you stare at the camera with a rictus smile of death, while your brain does handsprings in a desperate search for the exit. When people are kind enough to compliment me on my spontaneity or quick wit, I smile a quiet smile. It isn't complacency or engaging modesty;

BLEEDING AGAIN!

I'm remembering the stark terror of 'live' Irish television in its early days. Anybody who survived that, can survive *anything!*

        Time was, when being an announcer on RTE was the zenith of my ambitions. Then, as in every life, another ambition arises to supplant the old one: I sent a tape of a radio show I was presenting to the BBC. I didn't know anybody there, so I just addressed it to 'Gramophone Records Department'. I forgot to rewind the thing, so it arrived back to front. Mark White, on whose desk it landed, had the patience and sense of homour to rewind the tape, and listen. He offered me a series of 'Midday Spin', then 'Housewives Choice', which must have been okay, because when the pirates were finally sunk I was offered 'Late Night Extra' on the all-new, exciting Wonderful Radio One! For two years, I must have been the most-travelled disc-jockey in the world. Every Wednesday, I would introduce an Irish radio show, fly to London, introduce 'Late Night Extra' and fly back to Dublin in time to do another radio show there. 'Late Night Extra' was a marvellous, stimulating show to present, a mixture of pop, interviews, news, games and whatever excitements the night held. It was worth every long minute spent in the terminals, on buses and in cheap hotels.

Then, by cracky, the moment you've all had cause to regret. The biggest success on the new network, Radio One, was an already-aged crooner called Jimmy Young. This old chap was in sore need of rest, and another dose of Dr Frankenstein's electrodes, so Mark White asked me to bridge the gap. From that, I was offered the afternoon show on Radios One and Two. I upped stakes, wife and child, and here I am. . . .

The past eleven years can't have been much fun for you, dear listener and viewer, but they've been marvellous for me. I've done everything on radio from 'Any Questions' to 'Pop Scene', from 'Quote, Unquote' to 'Rosko's Round Table'. I've linked the Olympic and Commonwealth Games coverage, and had my own Radio Four chat show. On television I've endured the rigours of 'Miss World', 'A Song for Europe', 'The Eurovision Song Contest', 'Come Dancing' (I introduced that for seven years, and to this day, the British Public are still convinced it was Peter West), 'What's On Wogan', 'You Must Be Joking', 'Blankety-Blank', and other epics too numerous to mention here. I'd rather not talk about them anyway, if you don't mind.

But the most important date of all for me was April 1972, when I took over the 'Morning Show' from 7 to 9am on Radio Two. Lots of people in the business, and a number of critics, said I wouldn't make it, that I was 'wrong' for the morning, that the public wouldn't accept me. They were quite right, of course, but like the constant drip that I am, I have worn down their resistance. I'm still hanging on grimly, limpet-like, in the now-forlorn hope of acclaim and approbation, humbly offering this slim, worthless volume as a token of my esteem, your honour.

One at a time, lads!

You can lecture a few, harangue a crowd, and incite a multitude, as every demagogue since ancient Athens has known, but you can only *talk* to one person at a time. More than one, and it's a speech, and you run the risk not only of losing the attention of your additional listeners, but your original one as well.

If there's anything less riveting than a comedian analyzing what makes people laugh, it's a broadcaster trying to prove that there *is* somebody out there, hanging on his every word – but since you've stuck grimly thus far, indulge an old disc-jockey a mite further:

Any broadcaster who fancies that he is addressing the Great British Public every time the red light flashes on in his studio, is as a duck quacking in thunder (Confusius Mulligan, 'Madigan's Song', 1947). The concept of an 'audience' is a theatrical one; a large group of people gathered in an enclosed space, listening to the performance. Depending on that performance, the audience laughs, gasps, cries or throws rotten fruit *together*. One guffaw in the stalls can set the rest of the crowd chuckling. It's why opera stars used to employ 'claques' (maybe they still do!) to lead the cheering whenever they gave their tonsils an airing.

The audience for radio and television, on the other hand, consists usually of one or two people in a small room. Part of a huge national audience, certainly, but entirely separate from it. Nobody in Solihull laughs at the Two Ronnies simply because somebody in Gerrards Cross just did. They laugh if Corbett or Barker has said or done something that they, as individuals, find amusing. The radio listener and the television viewer make their own, personal evaluation of a performer or a performance without reference to the rest of the population, or even what their next-door neighbour thinks. Therefore, the listener and the viewer cannot be addressed *en masse* as though by the Pope from the Vatican pulpit, but as individuals. They can't be 'addressed', period. They must be spoken to, or for preference, with....

Nor can you be all things to all men. Nobody can speak with the one voice that all men will find acceptable. Just as there is no such thing as a universal sense of humour, there is no one point of view with which everyone can agree. It's a well-established precept that the honest broadcaster cannot open his mouth without offending someone, somewhere, usually in Scotland. My cheery 'Good morning' on a bright March day has

been greeted by torrents of abuse from irate Glaswegians pointing out tersely that it's chucking it down in Sauchiehall Street, and that the world does not end at Hampstead Garden Suburb....

Radio and television are 'one-to-one' media of communication; you're trying to establish contact with *one* listener, or *one* viewer. But who, I hear you cry, is this unfortunate, with whom I am trying to connect? Well, you can best establish a rapport with someone you instinctively like, someone who shares your sense of humour, your point of view, your tastes, your prejudices. You've got it. It's me. I'm talking to myself!

Whatever *some* of you may make of that, my view is that talking to yourself on the radio, or anywhere else, need not be such a bad thing. Look at it this way; don't you always try and talk sense to yourself? Don't you always give yourself credit for having *some* intelligence? People don't 'talk down' to themselves, they are usually honest at such moments, admit to their mistakes and shortcomings. Come on! Talk to yourself a little more – you might find out something to your advantange.

If, in talking with myself, I can establish a rapport, a meeting of minds with just *one* listener, then I'm doing it right. And it's a marvellous feeling to find someone on the same wavelength as yourself. There's a person called Pat Carr in Norwich who shares my sense of the ridiculous, but whose flights of fancy are only comparable to those of the Sainted Milligan.

You see, a report had come through of a sturdy Channel swimmer who claimed to have slept part of the way from Cap Gris Nez. I cast a little doubt on this, feeling, rightly or wrongly, that sleeping while swimming, or indeed swimming while sleeping, was a sovereign way to sink to the bottom like a stone. My comments provoked this, from the inestimable Carr:

Sir,

Following the news of this continental chappie swimming the Channel whilst still asleep I decided to be the first person to swim the Channel whilst chained to a lamp post in Birmingham.

Sadly, due to the swarms of greenfly we had recently sticking to the margarine covering my body, I was arrested as a sexual pervert on the M6. This was a fatal blow to my chances as by the time they got me and the lamp post into the patrol car I felt considerably weakened and as I cannot leave the country while still in jail I've had to postpone my attempt.

So would you cheer me up by sending best wishes to my wife, who is waiting for me in Calais with the key to the chains, and say 'Hurry home'.

This same great Carr was also inspired by the television epic 'Roots' and the story of the noble savage, Kunta Kinte, to recount the sad tale of 'Irish Roots' and Kunta Kinte O'Malley, who emigrated to Ireland during the Potato Famine, and opened a fish and chip shop! His speciality was cod and cos, an instant failure. Desperately, he experimented: spam fritters with thousands of peas, and a photograph of a chip. He tried a lucky dip, with a chip hidden in a 50-gallon bucket of mushy peas, all to no avail. His son was Fried Chicken George, who opened the first mackerel-fighting pits in Dublin. Huge bets were made, as two brave fighters stood in the pit hurling mackerel at each other. The first one to hold his nose was the loser.... It's a long tale, nearly as long as the original 'Roots', but I'll spare you it, on the basis of How Much More Is The Ordinary Man In The Street Expected To Take?

Quackers, or Mallard Imaginaire

It is in my capacity as honest broker for the self-same Ordinary Man In The Street that I cast the occasional aspersion on those who would delude the Great British Public, and lead them into schism and doubt. When last winter was at its dankest and dreariest, some doubtless well-meaning fan of our feathered friends put forward the general notion that whatever the weather, a man's best friend was his duck, and furthermore, these gifted little birds repaid observation in the matter of weather forecasting. I poured scorn on the whole idea, of course, being a seaweed man myself. How wrong I was! The next post brought a mildly admonitory letter from the Duck Observer at the Met. Office:

Dear Sir,
Of course it is difficult, for the ordinary man in the street, to understand how a duck can be any use to us at the Met. Office in these days of instant satellite pictures, and computers that can analyse weather reports and predict rain up to five hours before it happens. But I can assure you when it comes to really long-range weather forecasting, we still have to rely on the duck. Take for example the long hot summer of '76: the computer was forecasting snow storms throughout June. But Harry the Met. Office duck was conforming to this old rhyme, for that month:

June
If your duck goes ballroom dancing
Swallows you will soon be glancing.
But if your duck throws off his sequins
A freak frost will do your beans in.

I don't have to tell you we couldn't keep Harry off the dance floor that month. Funnily enough, a similar thing happened last year. If you remember, August was a very wet month, and if it hadn't been for Harry we at the Met. Office would have been left with egg on our face.

August
If your duck eats crisps with Guinness
It's lovely weather for playing tennis.
But if your duck throws down the packet
Forked lightning will hit your racket.

Sadly, due to the government's cuts, we've had to cease the long-range forecast. But we're hoping to transfer Harry to the twenty-four-hour forecast. So if you see a bulge in Michael Fish's trousers, you'll know it's only Harry, giving a last-minute report.

Pat Carr,
Duck Observer,
Met. Office.

It's Michael Fish's *jackets* that rivet my attention, not his trousers....
                        After that letter of course the Duck Lore flowed thick and fast:

***D**ear Ducky,*
It's not just the duck you have to watch to assess the weather –
drakes come into it too, you know. An old country saying goes like
this:

If your drake a duck do court,
Winter will be sharp and short.
Should 'ee preen whilst on the wing,
Thee should 'ave an early spring.
Should 'ee mate a mallard duck
Summer will be 'ot wi' luck.
But if your drake an egg do lay,
Then fetch the vet in right away.

Betty Collyer,
New Addington,
Croydon, Surrey.

I was invited to Adopt-a-Duck, which I have, and the game little bird bears the proud name of 'Platterpuss'.
                        I didn't have long to wait for something from the Duck Centre of Britain:

***D**ear Terry,*
Re: Ducks
As you know Aylesbury is noted for its duck population. At the
last census there were five of them! And they, for their own security,
live on the Police Station Pond. The wily Aylesbury Police are able
to detect the weather from careful observation of the ducks' habits.
The Chief Super whilst in his cups one night let the following
rhyme slip which I have never forgotten:

Be I Berks or be I Bucks
To check the weather I watch me ducks
Tails up high and not held down

Weather good and we'll get down
If they all clamps down their tails
Chin straps on, 'twill soon be gales.

John Hale,
Aylesbury, Bucks.

I leave the final word to the suitably named Bill Waddell:

Dear Mr Widgeon,
Re. Meteorological Ducks
In my recent work, 'The Maladjusted Mallard and Society', I
included a few old saws from the toolshed of folklore. Here are
some examples relating to forecasting:

If your duck do bite you twice
'Tis certain that there will be ice

If your duck stamp on your toe
You can expect a fall of snow

If your duck do break your knees
The wind will whistle through the trees

If your duck do punch your mouth
The soft wind bloweth from the south

If your duck do kick your nethers
You probably won't care what the weather's.

Bill Waddell,
Prestwick.

The first Eskimo

Weather being the national obsession that it is, during this
year's mild January I received countless letters from well-
meaning people bidding me join them in glorious celebration of
their early-blooming antirrhinums and hollyhocks. Pressed
flowers arrived in profusion with every post, and in short I was up
to my oxters in withered daffodils, daisies and winter roses. And I
must say, a pretty show they made around Denis O'Keefe's
headstone 'The dead producer'.

All this mild hysteria could only end in tears, and
things began to take a turn for the worse when Rebecca of
Sunnybrook Farm wrote in late January to tell me that she had
seen a sparrow carrying nest-building material in its beak!
Nothing was more calculated to set my listeners baying at the
moon; they began to hear cuckoos, see swallows, and sunbathe.
The competition was afoot to 'see the *first*' something – anything.

I had already noted the Regent Street shopkeepers starting their January sales in mid-December, then came a raft of letters on the first sightings of an Easter egg (early February, Streatham), of hot-cross buns (slightly later, Bradford). The first Christmas decorations were spotted in Bristol in the same month – the argument about whether these were merely last year's tinsel that hadn't been taken down, rages still. Several listeners reported the first sightings of an ice-cream van (January, all over the place).

The whole unsavoury business was, as usual, getting out of hand, until stopped in its tracks by a 'first' to end them all, from Jack Allen:

Dear Terry,
I'm writing to report another 'first'. Early yesterday morning I looked out of the bedroom window and there, crouching at the bottom of the garden, was my FIRST ESKIMO! Imagine my delight this very morning to discover there were now two of them and, although it was difficult to see through the driving snow, it looked very much as though they were starting to build an igloo!
This is very much earlier than last year and I'm hoping it's the same couple, as the wife, Nell, is a very good sort and was extremely popular at our local Rugby Club parties.

Jack Allen,
Fordingbridge, Hants.

Restores your faith, somehow, doesn't it?

NANOOK OF THE SOUTH

The search for Lawrence, or 'Hold that Camel!'

They're a literary lot, my crowd. Olivia Newton-John, or some other group, has only to release a record called 'Xanadu' for a torrent of bad jokes about 'Alph', the sacred river, to descend on my head. And poor old Samuel Taylor Coleridge! He gets seven bells knocked out of him:

Dear Terry,
I was listening to the Prog. this morning and managed to hear the bit about Khubla Khan over the noise of children charging about looking for their school books, etc. Here is my version of the famous pome – which I must confess I'd never heard before!

In Xanadu did Khubla Khan
Wonder where the lights had gone.

Shining brightly thro' the night
They must have been a wondrous sight.

Too bad the Union was on strike
When Khubla entered on his bike.

He might have seen the lady in black
Before she slapped a ticket on his back.

'Can't park there, it's not allowed,'
Then she vanished in the crowd.

From Xanadu rode the ruffled Khubla
Tooting loudly on a Tuba.

Enid Batchelor,
Eastbourne, Sussex.

In passing I was foolish enough to mention the Four Horsemen of the Acropolis – Moustaki, Mercouri, Mouskouri and Demis Roussos ('Throw another plate on the floor, Demosthenes!') – only for Mrs H. Carrington to let fly:

The Four Horsemen of the Apocalypse
Dismounted close by the Acropolis.
By the sight they were stirred,
Knowing not they incurred
One of Wogan's verbal atrocities!

Mrs H. Carrington,
Halesowen,
West Midlands.

I blame the educational system since the war, of course....
Then, just as I was about to nod off in the middle of a Manly Barrilow record, came 'Sons and Lovers'. This epic was serialized on television, and was mainly remarkable for the fact that the Son appeared to be a good deal older than his Mother. Since the subject of the great Lawrence had come up, I decided to show off a bit and opined that 'The Seven Pillars of Wisdom' was also a mighty piece of work, particularly when you consider how much time Lawrence spent riding his motorbike about the streets of Nottingham, and indeed, freeing the Arabs from Turkish thraldom, with only a camel and a white burnouse. Suddenly, the BBC switchboard was jammed – that person in the white frock was *never* D.H. Lawrence! It was *Gertrude!!* Oh yeah? Not according to Tony Martin:

Dear Mr Wogan,
Your correspondent is mistaken in asserting that the Middle-
Eastern person in the 'posh frock' was Gertrude Lawrence. The
person concerned was in fact the famous nurse known to all as
'The Lady of the Lamp' or Florence of Arabia.

For the record, Gertrude Lawrence was a famous
actress who played the part of Julie Andrews in the musical 'Seven
Pillars of Wisdom for Seven Brothers' by Richard Rodgers and
D.H. Lorenz Hart.

I trust this makes everything suitably obscure.
Tony Martin,
Halifax.

Which is as maybe – but as it turned out, nearly *everybody* was
wrong:

Dear Wog,
I would like to establish the following facts, once and for all, for the
benefit of your less educated listeners who daily
attend their transistors for that reason, ie to become
educated.

'Sons and Lovers' was written by David
Herbert Lawrence (1885–1930) and not Thomas
Edward Lawrence (1888–1935). They were in
fact half-brothers, D.H.
Lawrence's father being

a commercial traveller for the Coal Board in Eastwood in Dottigubshire and making many business trips to Wales where T.E. Lawrence was born and was later to become legendary as Lawrence of Arabia where he rode the desert on his thoroughbred camel dodging bombs and bullets and cursing in Classical Greek. It was ironic that he was killed in the country lanes of Dorset riding his father's old Coal Board motorbike which by that time, of course, had done many thousands of miles and needed servicing.

I hope that your listeners are now quite clear which Lawrence is which. If there is one thing which galls me, it is a distortion of the facts.

Jock Strapper,
3A Padded Cell,
Somewhere-cum-Oxford, Oxon.

Well, thank heaven that's all cleared up....

The show without a name

I like to think that if posterity remembers me for anything, it will be as a dispenser of sweetness and light, a Pollyanna of the airwaves, a Rebecca of Radio 2, one who ever sought the bluebird of happiness, the chink of light in the gloom. Who else sees merry commuters link their hands and march up Regent Street to the jolly strains of 'Sing As We Go!' Which is why it comes as a body-blow, when one enters the hallowed studios of the BBC ready for the challenge of a new day with a song bubbling away in the old breast, to pick up a letter that starts:

'**D**ear Mr Woburn,
I usually listen to Radio 3, but I haven't been very well lately; I think your Abbey is wonderful...'

or

'Some weeks ago I found that I was listening to your programme, by accident, I must admit...'

or, on return from holidays, open-countenanced and full of the joys of spring:

Dear Terry,
Look, I would have loved to be the first to welcome you back, but how can I lie?

While you were away, the family left punctually for their various destinations every morning, the cat came in and went out at regular intervals, we won a fortune on the horses, the clocks ticked in perfect synchronisation...

And now...
Jackie Jackson,
President of SPOTS,
(Stop Picking On Terry
Society),
Birkenhead, Merseyside.

Very nice. I'm supposed to have *no* feelings, of course. Ah, me. Then from 'Somewhere in Scotland' came:

*D**ear Terry,*
Please would you put the enclosed postcard in your hat. Not like a fishing fly – you know what I mean. I have to send it under cover in case the postman mocks me. You see I am a member of People Who Pretend They Never Listen To Terry Wogan And Even If They Did Wouldn't Dream of Writing To Him For Goodness Sake! or PWPTNLTTWAEITDWDOWTHFGS! for short. If I ever win a TWITS teeshirt I shall have to wear it in the privacy of my home, like when I had a pair of hot pants but always wore a coat over them in case anyone saw my legs.

I had a nasty moment the other day when I was about to struggle out in foul weather to post a letter to you. The minister called, and as he was leaving he offered to post it for me. I had to bluff him with merry shouts of, 'I love to walk in sleet and Force 9 gales, don't you?' and then set off bravely, bent double against the storm and in the wrong direction as the suspicious reverend gentleman drove off in the right direction, ie towards the nearest post box. Still, he probably thought I was doing something devious, which is better than something daft, or is it? I shall now put on my Groucho glasses, nose and moustache and my balaclava and post this.
I wish to remain eponymous.
Love and kisses, KT.

To paraphrase dear Oscar: 'Mine is the show that dare not speak its name.'

Every cloud...passes by

Then, just when you are beginning to question the very meaning of it all, to doubt the wisdom of carrying on, just at the moment when you're ready to lay your burden down, come the straws that finally did for the unfortunate camel – starting with some 'Converbs' from Patricia Craven of Canvey Island:

Every cloud has a soggy lining.
It's always darkest after night falls.
A stitch in time is a pain in the side.
Red sky in the morning, early warning. Red sky at night, too late.
Ne'er cast a goat 'til the light's gone out.
You can't have your cake and be a size 10.
As you sew, so shall your buttons fall off.

The demented Allison Walker-Morecroft of Worksop appended some 'Rules of Thumb' just to keep the spirits down:

The ladder is always in the other leg of your tights.
You take the dog out at the crack of dawn, when no-one is about. Wearing your old dressing gown and slippers you meet the postman, the milkman and the nosy next-door neighbour.
You change queues in the post office and get behind a man who taxes 10 cars.
You wait in all day for a telephone call: you go down the garden for a bit of parsley, and the 'phone rings.
You snuggle down in bed, to listen to your favourite DJ, at 7.30 am. There is a power cut. It comes on again at 9.55.

Just in case there was anyone left, unable to identify disaster when it struck, came these definitive words from Pauline Lynch of Great Yarmouth:

You know it's going to be a bad day when:
You wake up face down on the pavement.
You put your bra on backwards and it fits better.
You call the Samaritans, and they're engaged.
Your birthday cake collapses from the weight of the candles.
The woman you've been seeing on the side, begins to look like your wife.
You wake up to find your water bed is leaking – then you realize that you haven't got a water bed.

Your horn sticks on, as you follow a group of Hell's Angels down the motorway.
You reach out to put on the clothes you wore home from a party – and they're aren't any.
Your twin forgot your birthday.
Your child says: 'Did you know it's almost impossible to flush a grapefruit down the toilet?'

Auntie Wendy

Yet, there is much quiet satisfaction to be gained from helping the lame dog, fulfilling the long-felt want, answering the cri-de-coeur, the low moan of distressed gentle-folk. In my capacity as the Marje Proops/Claire Rayner of the airwaves, I reach out a helping hand to those in need of succour:

Dear Auntie Wendy,
Could you help me with my problem? As we have a rather large garden, I have recently employed the services of an odd-job man. He is a rather rough fellow, not at all educated in the social graces, by the name of Mellors.

Just lately he has become rather familiar with me. I must admit I am rather taken by his uncouth manner. He has a very furtive imagination, in fact, the things he can do with a forget-me-not have to be seen to be believed.

However I am worried about my husband finding out, but I really don't want to upset Mellors as we all know how difficult it is to get domestic staff these days.

I dare not reveal my true identity so I'm writing under my nom-de-plume of:

Pauline Lynch

Dear Auntie Wendy,
I am only 14, and madly in love with a handsome young man. Our parents have been at loggerheads for years and my mum wants to marry me off to someone else. I'm locked in at night, but my boyfriend comes into our garden and I lean out of the bedroom window to talk to him, while my friend Emily keeps watch. I'm really crazy about him, Auntie Wendy, and I've arranged to meet him in his father's orchard and we're going to be married. Emily says it'll all end in trouble.

What do you think? Please help.

Juliet Capulet,
Verona.

Rightly or wrongly I always feel that these simple tales of sundered hearts and unrequited passion don't need an answer from me. It's enough that I'm there as a kind of lightning

Dear Juliet

Your friend Emily sounds a drag. What you have there is a great idea for a play. Let me put you in touch with my Literary Agent...

AUNTIE WENDY

conductor, or, if you like, waste-pipe....

Some months ago, I was able to help Marje Proops herself find a missing couple with whom she wanted to spend a second honeymoon; for reasons best known to herself. Pretty unwholesome business, it seemed to me, but it prompted this letter:

*D*ear Terry,
On 24 December 1957, supermarket shopping for some Christmas goodies, I was at the check-out when a large middle-aged lady, dressed in an Ascot-type flowered hat, green jumper, red skirt and wellington boots pushed past me. In doing so, she rammed her elbow into my solar plexus, trod on my corn, and knocked a one-pound packet of split lentils out of my basket. The packet burst as it hit the floor. I stooped to pick up the débris and she said: 'Get out of my way, you clumsy oaf!'

I do hope that you can find the lady because I've just thought of a crushing rejoinder.

Jimmy Murray,
Watford.

I don't know about you, but in the matter of crushing rejoinders, ripostes such as the following can be most effective:

'Your grandfather's moustache!'

or

'So's your auld man!'

They rarely come back after a couple of shots like those.

Give the woman on the bed more porther!

After the ritual playing of hooligan music it is customary to shout a time-honoured slogan which, in the days of Alvar Liddell, John Snagge and Lord Reith, was thought to have a placatory effect on Aurum (The Ear in the Sky), the god of broadcasting. No such outmoded belief has currency these days, of course – although some Radio 3 announcers still cleave to the ancient custom of wearing a necklace of garlic when broadcasting after midnight – but the venerable slogans live on, each in its accustomed place. A piece of down-home, corn-pone, cracker-barrel country music must always be introduced by a high-pitched 'Eeee-Hah!', and finished off with any one of the following:

'Dang Ma Britches!'

'Set a Spell, and Let Your Saddle Cool!'

or

'Hand me the Spittoon, Jake – Phutt! – Missed Again!'

A sensitive performance of a Dixieland jazz epic must needs be greeted by the simple chant:

'Oo-yah! Oo-yah!'

A romantic ballad, when sung by a lady requires:

'Touch Me Not, Me Name's Temptation!'

'I am Promised to Another, You Shameless Hussy!'

or

'I'll give You 24 Hours to take Your Hand off My Knee…'.

A heart-rending tear-jerker, particularly when intoned by the ilk of Bobby Goldsboro or Vikki Carr, is invariably introduced thus:

'This'll Drain You of All Emotion'

or

'Here's one to Wring the Withers!'

Hearty party songs of the 'Do You Want Your Auld Lobby Washed Down?' type, must, of necessity, be properly finished off with the chant:

'Give the Woman on the Bed More Porther!'

The origins of this last are thought to date back through the mists of time, and out the other side, to the Firbolgo, an ancient Pre-Celtic race who were martyrs to the mead, and inclined to shout the first thing that came into their heads.…

The aforementioned shout is particularly effective when added to a manly drinking song, such as 'Hand Me Down That Bottle of Tequila, Sheila', sustaining, as it were, the imbibing motif.

Mind you, with its deep Mexican undertones, 'Tequila Sheila' ought, in the strictest tradition, to be greeted by quasi-Mexican incantations such as:

'Arriba, arriba – andele, andele'

or

'Ay-chihuahua!'

Or, in particularly extenuating circumstances:

'Remember the Alamo!'

Tequila-Sheila!

Anything to do with the good old demon drink brings them crawling out of the woodwork, trailing spotted pink elephants. I'm still trying to pass off on unsuspecting friends the sacks of 'Pina Colada Mix' heaped on me after I was foolish enough to play the 'Pina Colada' song, by Rupert Holmes.

In a moment of weakness, I happened to mention some of the favourite tipples in Dublin Working Men's Clubs, such as 'Smitwicks and Coke' or 'Pernod and White'. Arcane concoctions both, well up there in the cocktail stakes with *anything* the three witches in 'Macbeth' could do. Having undermined the moral fibre of the nation quite enough over the past few years, I refused to divulge the ingredients of these hell-brews to anyone.

However, one query persisted: what, in the name of all that's Holy, was 'White'?

I could scarce forbear to chuckle in a superior fashion. For isn't Ireland the only country in the known world with *two* colours of lemonade? One 'Red' – the other 'White'.

It is the mark of the eejit and gobdaw to enter any Irish drinking establishment and order, say, a 'Vodka and lemonade'. Conversation stops, the barman stands, thunderstruck. After a good minute of unspoken panic, the tension eases and wiser heads prevail. What if you *haven't* got all your marbles? Everyone can't be a genius. The barman's eyes soften: 'And what colour would you be wantin'?' he asks sympathetically. It's the stranger's turn to panic: 'Colour? What colour? Vodka has no colour!' 'No sir, the lemonade.' 'Lemonade? Lemonade? Lemonade has no colour....'. And so on far into the night.

I should, of course, have known better than to assert on the air that Ireland was the only country to boast two varieties of lemonade. Within hours, I was inundated with lemonade of every hue and colour of the rainbow, from the 'Golden' of Yorkshire, to the 'Tartan' (!) of Scotland. They only sent me the label from the latter – a pity, I'd dearly love to try a glass of tartan-coloured lemonade.

'Hand me Down that Bottle of Tequila, Sheila' suggested a range of catch-phrases, such as:

ARE YOU SURE YOU WON'T JOIN ME IN A GIN AND ANGOSTURA, MEIN FUEHRER?

'Another glass of Champagne-Perry, Terry?'
'Care for a Tia Maria with your Beer, Wazir?'
'How about a Rusty Nail, Abigail?'
'A glass of Sauterne, Ern?'
and best of all:
'Try the Syrup of Figs, Ronnie Biggs –
It'll keep you on the move...'

The line in the 'Tequila' song that foxed even the hardened drinkers was 'Pass me the salt and the lemon'. From the depths of my wisdom and drunken knowledge, I made a passing attempt at enlightening the ignorant, but luckily, help and guidance were at hand:

Dear Mr Wogan,

As a denizen of Cheadle Hulme with strong transatlantic links, I have been most fortunate in having received first-hand training in putting away Tequila Shooters, a drink whose description you chose to mangle this morning.

To set the record straight you need the following ingredients:

A bottle of tequila, and a glass
A small mound of salt
A lime (for which a lemon is but a poor substitute) in quarters.

First you put a pinch of salt on the back of one hand and a slug (that being the technical term for a double measure) of tequila in the glass. Lick the salt, drink down the slug of tequila in one go, and then, quickly, bite into the quarter of lime.

You then continue by licking a pinch of lime off your hand, downing the tequila and biting a quarter of salt. Then you put some tequila on your hand, drink a salt of lime, and bite into a slug.

Then you put salt on the slug, lick the tequila in your quarters, and bite into the back of your hand....

Cheers

Maurice Warwick,
Cheadle Hulme, Cheshire.

BBC fevers

The extempore effusion is no stranger to my morning macedoine. However, unlike the poet of yore, my listener needs no reason or romantic trauma to let fly with a burst of verse. I happened to quote freely from good old Wordsworth W. one morning, and got this by return of post

Lament for a one-time DJ

He wondered, as lonely as a cloud,
If there was someone there to hear,
For often, when he joined a crowd
The others used to disappear;
Predictably (though rather rude)
They left him in his solitude.

And oft, when burbling on the air
There was not one to answer back;
And this became too much to bear,
And caused his worried mind to crack;
And now you'll find him on the hills,
Conversing with the daffodils.

Lake District for the holidays?

Joan Wells,
Benfleet, Essex.

All I'm saying is, it takes one to know one, and they're not all locked up yet...Not content with that piece of well-turned calumny, Joan Wells let her gasping victim have another couple of staves straight in the mazzard:

IS ANYBODY OUT THERE...?

You are old, Terry Wogan, no doubt about that,
And your voice is quite manly and gruff;
And yet you incessantly talk through your hat –
Where d'you get such ridiculous stuff?

'In my youth,' he replied, 'I was awfully bright,
And I got it all out of me head;
But as long as the listeners continue to write
I'll use all their rubbish instead.'

A good foul slur, I agree, but knowing Wells of old, I was
expecting it. I was halfway through *this* merry little sonnet before
I realized what was going on:

Every morn across the nation
Waits an eager population,
Taut with anxious expectation
Oozing mindless adulation,
Cherishing their guiding slogan:
'Breakfast time means Terry Wogan.'
Hushed the bacon's fragrant sizzle,
Stilled the kettle's dying fizzle,
Snap, crackle, pop no longer heard,
'Eat quietly children, Mum's the word!'
Let not those dulcet tones so dear
Be lost, let everyone give ear,
The simpering sage of Radio 2
Pretentious prattle brings to you.
From half-past seven till ten o'clock
Our anti-hero runs amok.
On television too he bleats
To faithful forms slumped in their seats
And loyal listeners on the air
Agog each trenchant phrase to hear,
Of dogs and cones and walky-walkies,
Dallas, JR and all things mawkish.
How do I know these things are true?
Well, I've caught Woganism too!

Convalescent,
Fleet, Hampshire.

Bit like a knife in the small ribs, eh? You're dead for a half hour before you realize it. As I've said, the slightest thing can set the listener off: last summer, as is the BBC Heating Engineer's wont, the radiators were going full blast on the warmest day of the year (naturally, in the depths of winter the heating is switched off). I mentioned that it was a good job that I had my solar topee, fly whisk and water-carrier with me, and invited the listener to hearken for the merry chirp of the cicada, and keep a wary ear out for the message of the talking drums. I'm pretty certain the far-away trumpetings of the elephant herd were audible, and to my certain knowledge Tarzan himself swung through the studio on a couple of occasions.

       In a word, I went well over the top – but heat can do strange things to a man, as Denise Hulme, from the steaming Potteries, understands:

*Down in the jungle basement of the good
ole' BBC
Wogan sits sweltering beneath the banyan
tree*

*Alligators snap their teeth, parrots swoop
and call
Monkeys swinging from the trees, giraffes
elegant and tall*

*In among this chaos our intrepid DJ man
Broadcasts his morning programme minus
extractor fan*

He follows after Brandon has been there
and done his stint
And bravely risks his everything, of
complaint there is no hint

In safari coat and topee hat he sits without
a murmur
(We know that he is AOK, he trained for this
in Burma)

Bush Rangers drive past now and then in
vans striped black and white
Shooting old rogue elephants, rampaging
through the night

Our Terry sits there through all this and
now and then exclaims
'My God this heat' and 'What a smell, it
must be the old drains'

It's air he needs, some oxygen, a fan to
ventilate
So fellow TWITS have sympathy with our
poor Wogan's fate.

Denise Hulme,
Stoke-on-Trent.

There – somebody cares – it gives a body a warm glow, which
if you're not very careful with my lot can turn like a flash
into a high temperature – a BBC Fever!

(With apologies to John Masefield)

I must tune-in to the Beeb again,
To that august voice from the sky.
So what I need is a radio,
The better to hear it by.
And all I ask is a 'TWITS' T-shirt*
And a Radio Two type sponge;
'Cos it's time for my annual bath again,
And I'm going to take the plunge!

I must tune-in to the Beeb again,
To the Terry Wogan show.
At O-Seven-Thirty I'll steel myself
And switch on my radio.
And all I ask is a pair of plugs
To bung into my ears;
Otherwise I'll go 'Beresk'
And then burst into tears!

I must tune-in to the Beeb again,
The home of the great DG
And if he offers a sacrifice
He'll get applause from me.
All preparations being in hand
Six acolytes take JY,
And hurl him over the parapet
To that studio in the sky!

I must tune-in to the Beeb again,
For news of JR Ewing.
And learn, from Terry's honeyed lips,
What sinister plots are brewing.
And hear if 'Mangy Bendy-Toe'
And 'The Nolan Brothers' too,
Have laid-down any brand new songs
To sing for me and you!

I must tune-in to the Beeb again,
To hear if you'll read this poem.
And if you don't,
It's to another station I'll be going.
Radio One's too R & B,
And Radio Four's too boring.
So it looks as though it's Radio Three
My custom will be scoring!

Jan Swales,
Skegness, Lincs.
*Chestal area 37in.

Is it any wonder that Sir John Betjeman quivers like a jelly in his floral-patterned wellington boots?

Eat up, you're at your Grannie's

Plonked as I am, in the middle of the Great British Breakfast, it's no wonder that a sizeable chunk of my mail is about food. It's a pretty free-ranging topic, from irate brigadiers, fulminating against the poor quality of today's back rasher, to equally irate mothers raging at the adhesive qualities of porridge, particularly when stuck to the ceiling. If I'm any judge, Breakfast with Britain is a madstorm, a cacophony of screaming children, demented dogs, and snarling grannies, while through a haze of flying wheatybangs can be seen the barely discernible form of another British mother having a fit in the corner. 'A merry prospect,' you cry, and so do I, especially when viewed from a great distance. I have long held that what holds my marriage together is the simple fact that I have escaped to work before the living hell of Family Breakfast at Wogan Towers begins.

I SAID, TURN THAT THING DOWN – I CAN'T HEAR MY FLAKIPUFFS!

As you may know, or if you don't you soon will, I am often asked for succour and advice on all manner of problems: the sundered heart, the missing cat, the first cuckoo – matters of impact and social significance. In that capacity, as arbiter of correct social deportment and behaviour (who was it insisted that porridge was to be eaten not only upright, but on the move?) I was recently asked to hand down a considered judgment on the matter of meals, their timing, appellation, and correct mode of ingestion! What, they cried, was the difference between lunch, dinner, high tea and supper? Where did a tray come in? And *when* should they all take place?

Even one as keenly aware of modern social modes as myself was be-flummoxed. Luckily the gentry came up trumps – witness this definitive work from Ralph Montagu, of a certain Palace at Beaulieu, Hants.

Breakfast

There is no other name for this meal which is served from 2am at parties through to around 10am. It is not modern etiquette to eat standing.

Lunch or luncheon

Is only eaten around midday, preferably on the dot of 1 o'clock. If it is your main meal of the day it is theoretically correct to call this meal 'dinner' although this is not generally the done thing.

HANG IT ALL, CARSTAIRS – I'M TOO BIG STILL TO BE HAVING DIN-DINS AT MIDDAY!

Tea

This may be any meal served between about 4 and 6.00. It may take various forms from simply tea and biscuits, to jelly, ice cream and cakes at parties, to a 'high tea' (this term is largely out of date) which constitutes a small main course such as egg and chips or sausages and mash followed by bread and butter, toast, fruit or cheese and biscuits. High tea is commonly served at boarding schools in the evening. The earliest tea is probably available from British Railways Southern Region when tea and high tea are first served on the 2.35pm Waterloo – Bournemouth train (and a good tea it is too.) It is still common practice for caterers to use the term 'high tea' although you would not expect to hear it in all but the most out-of-date homes.

Supper

This is a meal eaten in the evening after around 6.30 and should consist of at least two full courses. If it is eaten formally after 8 o'clock it can only be because lunch is your main meal of the day. Supper could well be eaten off a tray in the sitting or drawing room or bedroom, even if it is your main meal of the day. The word supper is derived from 'soup-er.'

Dinner

This is always the main meal of the day, although if eaten at midday it should be called lunch except perhaps by children who only have a large tea in the evening. Dinner should be eaten in the dining room and you should change before. You would expect at least three if not four or five courses.

P.S. My father insists on having high tea before going to the cinema or theatre.

That certainly cleared things up for us middle-class with pretensions, but was the Plain-Spoken-Man-In-The-Street to go unheard? Are you kidding?

Dear Mr Wogan,

For goodness sake let a Lancashire lass put you right about mealtimes. These Southerners know nothing about it!

Breakfast is a meal nobody can afford any more.

Lunch is elevenses or dinner at midday if you're trying to be posh.

Dinner is what you have at lunchtime or in the evening only if announced by a gong.

Tea is dinner (or lunch) at teatime, or a drink.

High tea and low tea on the lawn are only in books.

Supper is a butty before you go to bed.

OK?

Madalaine Brady,
Bangor, Gwynedd.

Look, fight it out amongst yourselves. Anyone hear a tumbril?

What is this strange power?

I have already drawn your attention, dear reader, to the strange power I have over women. If not, I must be slipping.... Of the thousands of examples of my Rasputinian powers that spring to mind, let one suffice to hammer the homily home.

Dear TW,

I want you to know that I object most strongly to you making the Nation concentrate on me winning a race at 3.35 today. I look (and feel) ridiculous tearing down the High Street with my shopping trolly flying behind me.

Mrs (Joyce) Penny,
Andover, Hampshire.

You see, in a moment of high desperation, with a list of losers as long as your arm behind me, I had implored the Great British Punter to get behind a horse called Mrs Penny. I felt that if there was anything at all in this 'Power of Thought' business, the concerted brain-waves of four million listeners would be more than enough to impel a one-legged drunken tortoise first past the post in the Derby, not to mind this pampered thoroughbred in the 3.35 at Catterick. Mrs Penny, the horse, won, but it's a good job Mrs Penny, the housewife, wasn't anywhere near Catterick on the day, or it might have been a dead-heat!

I haven't tried the thought-transference ploy since then, lest I unleash similar uncontrollable forces on the nation, with great surges of brain-waves sweeping the country, driving before them any person or thing unfortunate enough to be synonymous with the selected nag. Once again, a thousand examples spring to my jaded brain, but let me simply offer you one – a horse called Mai Pussy. Can even the most robust among you let the mind dwell for more than a moment on the consequences?

Speaking, as we luckily were, of our carapaced chum the tortoise, even *his* sturdy shell is not proof against me:

Dear Terry,
My mum said that the BBC were getting rid of you and putting David Hamilton on instead. Is this true? I hope not because of my tortoise. If it wasn't for you, Terry, I would never be able to control Toby. Your early morning jokes and music send my Toby to sleep. My other tortoise Tulketh died through doing too much exercise when we didn't turn you on.

Alison Gray,
Southport.

I get a surprising number of letters about tortoises, mainly from people who make extraordinary claims for their little pets. Apparently the island is alive with tortoises that bite lumps out of the furniture, prey on cats and guests, cover the ground like greyhounds, eat steak and chips, drink whiskey and never hibernate. I'm never sure whether these tortoise-owners are writing for advice, or out of a spirit of boastfulness, but I usually content myself with the gentle speculation that they may be deluding themselves as to the nature of their pets. It seems patently obvious to one that these misguided folk may have in their possession snapping turtles, spiny anteaters, armadillos, alligators or, mayhap, the odd Tasmanian Devil, but what they haven't got is a tortoise!

The man with the budgie...
and other fishy business

If it all stopped with women and tortoises, of course, it would be alright – but it doesn't end there. The man in the street is confused. Not just by the Public Sector Borrowing Requirement, The Green Pound, VAT, tortoises, or women either. Such is his state of confusion and doubt that he can't tell a budgie from a St Bernard. Well, at least *one* man can't. He's the man who takes his budgie for a walk every day to the Robin Hood Roundabout in Birmingham. He stands there, letting his feathered friend breathe in the health-giving fumes, causing alarm, despondency and many a dented bumper among newcomers to the Robin Hood Roundabout, and arousing the protective instincts of the locals:

Dear Terry Wogan,
How dare you mock our 'budgie man.' What a bit of colour he puts into our lives!
I met him one morning whilst weeding my front garden and had a very long conversation with him. We talked about his budgie, a lively little thing swinging madly about on his

perch. He is a fellow sufferer of migraine (the man, not the budgie) and has given me his remedy. Mustard on the forehead! Every time I see him now he raises his cap and shouts at me: 'Have you tried it yet?'

Solihull would be a sad place without our friendly little budgie man with the yellow forehead, so desist your witticisms and try taking a bird for a walk yourself!

Jocelyn Gandy,
Solihull.

I'd had several sightings of The Budgie Man, but nobody had mentioned a *yellow forehead!* I had, perhaps, been a little unfair to the chap, and had suggested that it might be something other than a budgie in that cage – like a green chihuahua, or a stuffed capon. A denizen of Hall Green, Birmingham riposted swiftly:

D*ear Terry,*
Now this elderly gentleman who takes his green and yellow budgie for walks by the Robin Hood Island – he's been doing it for the last three or four years to my knowledge. He never takes it out on cold, wet days. The budgie (whom we call Norwich City in this family) loves his walks and sings and hops about. He is definitely not stuffed. His cage is always immaculate (unlike my lounge!). 'The man' will show his budgie to anyone who wants to see it, so with my five children always wanting to see anything, I can assure you that 'the man' is not a clone, leprechaun, garden gnome or anything sinister. I'm just sorry I've never actually asked him his name. So please don't say anything nasty about him – he always looks so happy with his little companion, I'd hate him to be upset.

Anyway, we need something round here to make us famous. We do not have a park, a swimming bath, a nursery school, a place where you can get a cup of tea or a Sainsbury's.
LATER
My friend has just seen him – 9.25am – down the Stratford Road.

Liz Docker,
Hall Green, Birmingham.

Spies everywhere. Speculation, as always on the Benighted Breakfast Blather, spread like wildfire bringing the wild-eyed loonies out from every nook and cranny of the West Midlands. Here's another sample:

Dear Terry,

INSIDE INFORMATION ON MAN WITH BUDGIE.
I too have seen the man with the budgie but unlike your previous correspondent I know why he's there and has been for at least two years.

He's employed by Sir Michael Edwardes as a Japanese car counter. He doesn't actually count the cars himself, the budgies do. He has a fresh budgie every morning well versed in Japanese car identification and budgicarsie, the gentle art of aiming itself from a height of exactly 15ft 7in into the windscreen of a Japanese car, if the amount of Japanese cars going round Robin Hood Island exceeds 47%. Little is known of his training methods

WHAT I SAY IS, IF IT'S GOT YOUR NUMBER ON IT...

HONDA

DLY 827W

*but I have seen him very close to Robin
Hood Cemetery on many occasions.
My personal opinion is that his budgies are
reincarnations of Lord Brabazon, who once had
a budgie and, as you well know, invented cars.*

*Keith Dutson,
Solihull.*

*P.S. I also have inside information on the whereabouts of Veronica
Lake and the Lady with the Bucket.*

Don't ask me about that P.S. There are some things into
which it is better not to inquire too deeply.
        Alan J. Holden of Wolverhampton seemed to
think that the M. with the B. might be his Uncle Andy, whom he
had carelessly mislaid at the Spaghetti Junction Lupin Festival,
while Steve Crenshaw was certain he knew the mystery man's
identity:

*D*ear Terry,
*The man on the traffic island. It's Jim Smith, manager of
Birmingham City, a sort of football club. You see they once had a
proper young footballer named Trevor Francis and Jim sold him
for a sack of gold and then used the gold to purchase some ageing
dummies and they're known as Dad's Army. So all the supporters
collectively gave him the bird and he has to wear it around his neck
like an albatross and he stoppeth one in three to tell his sad tale
and he cannot leave the island until B'ham City win the European
Cup.*

Steve Crenshaw.

Anyone detect the merest hint of bitterness? Then, from Wales,
the Celtic fringe lifted long enough to let another one escape:

*D*ear Terry,
*Taking a budgie or a sheep for a walk is nothing. I once knew a
man who used to take his goldfish for a walk. This took a lifetime of
training, and started by taking the fish out of the water for a few*

seconds at first and gradually increasing the time. As this was going on the water in the tank gradually reduced, until in the end the fish became totally 'oxygenised'.

As he left his front door every morning this man was heard to cry out in a true Barbara Woodhouse tone: 'Floppies!' and off they would go. However, after all this effort, tragedy struck one day. Whilst crossing a bridge the fish slipped the lead, fell into the river below, and was drowned.

Rupert Jenkins,
Swansea.

This, you hardly need the likes of me to tell you, opened the flood-gates for the Pisceans, or fish-fanciers:

*D*ear Terry,
So listeners have birds who think they are dogs! Have any, I wonder, got a bossy fish? When mine thinks it's time for a meal he comes to the side of the tank and stares at me as if to say: 'Hey, before you start on your evening meal what about mine?' Next comes the funny bit: should I ignore this preliminary request he waggles from side to side finishing with a vigorous nod of the head backwards, quite clearly saying: 'C'mon, over here or I'll come and sort you out'. This demand is impossible to ignore but should I continue with the business of getting our own meal ready, he then thinks he's a whale and does an enormous leap and broadside flop – water up the wall, all over the shelf and floor. Quite a character our Duffin, now 9 years old.

Any other fish would have been dead long ago. He has suffered the most incredible ordeals and recovered, like jumping out of his tank and lying on the kitchen floor all night and apparently dead for two days but recovered (horribly bruised) only to lose his tail and fins, but grew more. I won't go on, but fish have taken on a new dimension in my book.

Florence Burberry.

What the woman has there, of course, if fish at all, is a *flying* fish or possibly a dolphin. We must hope against hope that it isn't a killer whale, luring her into a false sense of security with a show of winsomeness. Florence Burberry's letter naturally gave rise to a number of racy tales of queer fish: guppies that did party-tricks in the sink, capering carp and goldfish that mimed to records or the wireless. Alan Cherrington had a fishy query:

Dear Mr Ownag,
Can a fish join Equity? I have been watching the angling programme, 'Hooked!', and I am sure that the same roach has been caught, three weeks in succession!

Last week I detected a trace of make-up around its little gills and the merest suggestion of a James Cagney impression. I blame the Russians!

Alan Cherrington,
Tamworth.

So do I, Alan, and more importantly so does the DG. Convinced that one day the Red Army tanks will roll down Regent Street, he lies in wait on the BBC ramparts with a cauldron of molten Jimmy Young records and a crate of Nolan Sisters, all of which he proposes to hurl upon the unsuspecting heads of the Mongol Horde.

You can't blame the Russians for everything, of course. It's hardly Brezhnev's fault that people confuse budgies with boxers, piranhas with parrots, tortoises with alligators and women with dogs. Come again? You heard me the first time. Have a gander at this:

Dear Terry Wogan,
Having watched Barbara Woodhouse training dogowners so forcibly and with such good results, I wondered if the dogs themselves were really necessary and had been added to give a little colour to the square of grass on which their owners paraded. Being sick and tired of my wife's erratic behaviour when I take her shopping, I thought I would try to cure her of dashing across the road to inspect bargains, or pulling me into shop doorways. I re-read the BBC book of the series 'Tickle Their Chests' and listened to the BBC record of 'The Dog-owner's Lament' and off we went to the High Street.

What a transformation! She absolutely loved the

clanking of the chain around her neck, and sat down so smartly on
command that she twice drew respectful applause from long-
suffering husbands trying to drag their wives away from sales
counters. With what ecstasy did I utter those four magic words:
'What A Good Girl.'

Unfortunately I was arrested by a policeman, who
hadn't watched Barbara Woodhouse, when I made the correct
friendly gesture outside Woolworth's.

Michael Ryan,
Penrith.

Heavens! I can see the letters to *Women's Guardian* now.
Ryan will probably get a whole Jill Tweedie column to himself.
The fur will fly, as do the feathers.

Kamikaze cockatiels

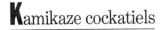

Two of which, feathers that is, I have before me e'en as we speak. Rather like the radio, you'll have to take that on trust, but believe me, me hearties, pretty poor specimens of plumage they make. They come from Carol Lyons of Lambeg, Lisburn, Northern Ireland, who first drew the already drained public's attention to the suicidal tendencies of cockatiels by describing the antics of her little Archie, who enlivens her Lisburn breakfast boredom by hurling himself, beak-first, into the porridge, and then, stunned, staggers all over the wallpaper, curtains and kitchen floor, leaving little porridgy cockatiel clawmarks in his wake.

Before we go any further (and don't think I haven't noticed you casting your eyes to heaven), let me explain that exhaustive inquiries, and pictures of the little rascals from helpful listeners, have led me to deduce that the cockatiel is a budgie-sized bird with pretensions to being a cockatoo. Think of the thing as a budgie with a headdress, and you won't go far wrong.

YOU CAN'T TALK TO GREGORY NOW HE'S JUST DROPPED OFF

Any road up, having received and read out Carol Lyons's letter, I speculated patronizingly that she might have the one and only Kamikaze Cockatiel in captivity, and left it at that, moving swiftly on to that pleasing baritone, Irish Williams and her Mongolian Nose-Flute, or some other plangent sound....

Useless to claim now that I should have known better. The next post brought a flurry of letters, eg:

Dear Terry,
I have a cockatiel whose name is Gregory (short for Gregory Peck). Frequently during the afternoon I don't have the radio on as the programme does not appeal to me so the house is quiet and Gregory (who is almost 20 years old) has a nap. However, if the telephone rings he is so startled he falls off the perch crashing on to

the floor of his cage. He immediately picks himself up, shakes his head, and starts shouting 'Hello, hello, hello' answering the telephone.

Marjorie Wedge,
Wolverhampton.

Old Gregory Peck sound a little ga-ga to me. There were several instances of barmy birds who crashed into the custard, mangled the marmalade and bashed the mashed potatoes, but Anne Jones had one of more exotic tastes:

Dear Terry,
I have an awful warning for eaters of tinned spaghetti. My beloved cockatiel Cholmondelay – pronounced as you well know Chumly (known as 'Chums') who was in his day a great pecker of unwary visitors' fingers, ears, or whatever was offered in a trusting fashion to his voracious beak – was strolling, or rather waddling, for cockatiels roll from side to side in a slightly drunken way, rather than place one foot in front of another in a respectable walk.
   He was waddling around my children's breakfast table, checking on the freshness of the cornflakes, shaking the occasional beakful of milk and sugar on the clean tablecloth, and pretending that he thought the fringe of the cloth was a particularly stubborn enemy to be destroyed. He suddenly took a right turn and slushed straight through the tinned spaghetti on my daughter's plate.
   And here is where the warning becomes clear.
   He emerged the other side of the buttery toast and spaghetti with little fluorescent wellingtons on his feathery feet. The colour lasted for weeks. What do the makers put into their tins of spaghetti?

Anne Jones,
Witney, Oxfordshire.

P.S. I suppose he could have got a job, perched on a motorcyclist's shoulders as a night reflector.

Come on Anne – what's the use of blaming the tinned spaghetti for your beaked wonder's shortcomings? And as for the P.S! Have you ever seen Hitchcock's film 'The Birds'? I wouldn't be a bit surprised if you got beaten up by a gang of rooks.

But to return to those two dingy feathers I have before me, and the latest report I have on the benighted bird that started it all, from the plucky Miss Lyons:

Dear Terry,
I took Archie – the Kamikaze Cockatiel – home with me for Christmas.

When I went out on Boxing Day, my poor unsuspecting mother let him out, because his wings looked cramped, having been locked away since Christmas Eve.

He rewarded her by diving into the beetroot and onion, and then, whilst his little feet were all purple, tried to walk through my brother Geoffrey's dinner.

I brought him home in disgrace. Unfortunately now he has started to moult and perches in all sorts of weird positions, pulling out his feathers willy-nilly!

Since New Year's Eve, which he celebrated by swooping down on all my party guests, frightening them to death and landing on their heads, he has decided he is a dog. He struts about the floor – and all over me, as I try to do my Yoga – leaving his nasty little calling cards in very surprising places, like shoes, etc.

He was sulking about the sofa last night, and not being aware of his presence, I sat on him. There was a loud squawk, nearly scaring me silly, and he flew off, looking very put out, but fortunately (for him) unharmed. He now stays away from the sofa – the wise bird.

As you can see, he still eats letters, but so far he has refused to eat my electric bill. I must apologize for the state of this letter, you'd think he'd never been fed.

Carol Lyons and Archie,
Lisburn, Northern Ireland.

The letter *was* a little frayed, but who isn't these days? Particularly when you think of what's *really* going on behind the quiet facades of the nation's semi-detacheds....

Thank heaven, say I, for Pat Carr, and the voice of sanity:

D*ear Mr Wogan,*

As a cockatoo owner of many years' standing, I can truthfully state that I am totally mystified by these constant reports of cockatoos with suicidal tendencies.

Because Jeffrey, my pedigree cockatoo, has never flown around the room squawking and diving into my porridge, in fact he's never flown.

He does however constantly fall off his perch; but I always put this down to his webbed feet. And not any wish on his part to join his ancestors in the sky. I have since taken out that silly little perch the manufacturers of cockatoo cages will insist on using, and replaced it with a length of 4 x 2 plank. He hasn't fallen off since.

As for cockatoos using foul language, as stated by some of your listeners, I can only think they have been sold budgerigars by some backstreet pet shop swindler.

I've listed below a few simple guide lines which will enable any one with a suspect cockatoo, to establish its authenticity.

1 Does your bird A) say 'Who's a pretty boy then'; B) sing along with Kate Bush records; C) quack?

If your answer is A or B you have been swindled.
2 When you take your cockatoo for its morning walk does it A) slip its leash and dive into the nearest river till you manage to coax it out with a lump of bread; B) fly above your head swearing while you hold a piece of string tied to its leg; C) stand on your head eating a coconut?

If your answer is B or C I don't know what you've got but it certainly isn't a cockatoo.
3 When you give your cockatoo his weekly bath does he A) swim around quacking to his little friend Donald the rubber duck; B) bite a lump out of your nose and fly onto the bathroom door?

If your answer is B, don't panic, you're trapped in the bathroom with a flesh-eating African vulture, who hasn't had a square meal since you started feeding him on budgie seed six weeks ago.

Pat Carr,
Norwich.

LOVELY WEATHER FOR COCKATOOS!

The great putt

Nothing flatters my pathetic ego more than to be invited to play in the Pro-Celebrity golf series for BBC2 television. I suspect this is true of all of us in show business, radio or television who attempt to play golf. Which is why not only the home-grown little twinklers clamour to be included, but also pan-galactic luminaries of the calibre of Sean Connery, Jack Lemmon, Glen Campbell and Robert Stack are delighted to be asked.

Nobody gets a fee: we are content, in our simple way, to enjoy the Versailles-like delights of Gleneagles Hotel, its four golf courses, every creature comfort known to man, and the honour of playing with some of the world's greatest golfers. Every rabbit such as myself will understand the thrill I feel, as a bad 16-handicapper, to share a tee with the likes of Lee Trevino, Ben Crenshaw, Tony Jacklin and Fuzzy Zoeller!

Mind you, the thrill occurs in prospect and retrospect! On the great day itself, your breakfast is as ashes in your mouth, a terrible dryness affects the throat, the hands become clammy and as you stand on the first tee you can hear a distinct knocking – of your knees, going at it like a pair of maraccas. When I try to explain how nervous we 'celebs' feel on such an occasion, the tendency of the man in the street is to burst into a ribald chortle, and accuse me of making excuses for my pathetic scuffling up the fairway. But it doesn't matter how blasé and masterful you may be in front of a TV camera in your own bailiwick, being asked to strike a golf ball in the eye of a lens, with a gallery of hundreds and under the nose of Lee Trevino is an entirely different matter. Wondering what Peter Alliss is going to make of your dithering in the commentary doesn't exactly inspire confidence either. I have seen some of our greatest stars and sportsmen reduced to gibbering wrecks in the 'hostility' suite after one of these games, as they desperately try to justify missing a two-foot putt and explaining how, only the other day, they astounded friend and foe alike by burning up the 'Burma Road' at Wentworth.

Last year was my third Pro-Celebrity catharsis – why they had asked me back after the débâcle of the previous year, in which I had played in 'custard-yellow' trousers with all the consistency of a jelly, I'll never know. Something to do with my ineptitude making the average club golfer feel better about his own game, I expect. On that occasion I had played with 'gentle' Ben Crenshaw against Lee Trevino and Peter Cook, a match remarkable only for Cook's appearance, in full stage make-up, on the first tee. He took six putts on the first green, I took five, and only hope that you switched off after that.

My third appearance, would, I was determined, be different. I was going to be relaxed, and 'just enjoy the day', as all my friends advised. Har! Having played out of a bunker, I reached the first green in four. 'Okay partner,' murmured the sweet-natured Fuzzy Zoeller, 'just leg it up to the hole nice 'n easy.' The usual mist swam before my eyes, I hit the ground behind the ball and it moved all of a foot. Zoeller came up behind me again: 'You dumb......!' he muttered kindly, and fell to the green, laughing hysterically. It was more or less like this all the way around the King's Course, with old Alliss desperately trying to preserve the spirit of the Royal and Ancient, with encouraging phrases such as 'Golf is a serious game, lads'– all to no avail.

Then we came to the final green, the 18th, where a huge gallery had gathered to see our hero make an abject fool of himself, yet again. I was barely on the great green, about 33 yards from the hole, and the ever-encouraging Zoeller opined that I might well need my driver from there. I swung my putter, closed my eyes, and after about five minutes there was an enormous cheer. With all the green to roll on, the blessed little pill had finished up in the hole. Zoeller gave me the kiss of life, Trevino said it was the longest putt he had ever seen, and I'll swear I saw a little tear course down one of Alliss's apple cheeks.

In clubhouses up and down the country, wherever the great game is discussed, they still talk about that putt. Well, I do anyway; but you'll always get the begrudger, the bar-room cynic. A foul calumny has grown up around the Great Putt: the locker-room whisper is that it was all done by electronic chicanery. Imagine, if you will, my shock at this effusion from Bev Daily, a physician and one-time friend:

He really was bad at the eighteenth hole
And took seven shots on the green.
The TV producer got very upset
'This won't keep folks glued to the screen!'
So they took the tape to the video men
And said 'Now, just look at this berk,
He hit the ground, he missed the ball,
It's time you got to work.
He hit the ball past, he left the ball short,
The next shot he hit past again,

Then from six inches it rolled round the cup.
To watch it just gives you a pain!
So keep in the first shot he did from the edge,
And leave all the other ones out.
Splice them together – just leave in the ball,
Make it look like one mighty clout.'
So that's how it happened, this epic of sport,
By skill with the splice and the cut.
Some glue, fifteen pieces of separate tape
And they made up 'The Wogan Putt'.

Bev Daily,
Burnham, Bucks.

Ah, there, Bev. How much sharper than a serpent's tooth, etc., etc. They would even deny me my one far fierce moment of glory. Oh well, 'Sic transit Gloria Swanson', as Jack Nicklaus would say.

A tale of two lighthouses

Nostalgia, as the ancient wit put it, is a thing of the past, but it provides a powerful incentive for listeners to have a jolly good old wallow, as they recall the palmy, halcyon days of their youth. My daily 'Musical Memory' spot on the morning radio show gives them just such an opportunity: they divulge a racy secret from their seamy past, and I play the piece of music they request, to bring the old memories crowding back.

One woman recalled the extraordinary story of how she met her husband during the last war: she was, apparently, the driver of a 'mobile lavatory'. No, I hadn't heard of them either, but they were a vital part of the war effort, and a great source of comfort and relief, particularly to firemen, wardens and troops on manoeuvre. One night, after a bombing raid on Southampton, our heroine was driving her mobile loo back to base, with, as she delicately put it, a 'full load'. Rounding the corner of a quiet country lane, she ran straight into an RAF bus. Over went the mobile lavvy, with what results I can safely leave you to imagine.

As the game girl lay there stunned and, in the words of the song, 'Covered all over from head to toe, covered all over in ... sweet violets', a gallant, some would say foolhardy, RAF lieutenant picked her up and carried her to safety!

I NOW PRONOUNCE YOU MAN AND WIFE

She married him almost immediately of course. Well, wouldn't you? If that wasn't the ultimate test of true love, I've never heard it, and you can keep your Cyrano de Bergerac.

The 'Musical Memory' spot, as well as evoking marvellous stories, every so often throws up a request for some obscure record from the dim and distant past, which, as soon as it's played, provokes a huge reaction from the listeners. None more so than a record entitled 'The Lighthouse across the Bay'.

This remarkable ditty came from a movie of the '30s called 'No Reply from Floating Platform One', and was intoned with Teutonic precision by one of the stars of the film and one of the heartthrobs of his era, Conrad Veidt. It's impossible to convey in the written word the eccentricities of Veidt's English, but it certainly tickled the nation's fancy. The way the bold Conrad told it, the song was of a 'cottage, thatched with strroow' over which 'sea-gools' swooped, where stood a fair-haired 'lessee', 'stair-gazing'. Incidentally, in case you were lucky enough to have missed it, this cottage was also 'kissed by human spray'. Well, I think what was meant was 'fume and spray', but me and the gang preferred the 'human' variety.

The response to this unconsciously hilarious performance was immediate, enormous and multilingual:

I write in a Teutonic fury.
Donner und Blitzen I say
Desist from taking ze Michael
From my lighthouse across ze bay.

My housekeeper has twists in her knickers
And thinks you ought to atone,
I know she's a lighthouse keeper
She only goes six und half stone!

She spends most of ze time 'stair' gazing.
Amidst ze spume and ze spray
There's two hundred steps in my lighthouse
And she scrubs them, three times a day!

WHAT DO YOU MEAN, MY TEETH ARE LIKE STAIRS?

In her spare time she stands
by her cottage,
Peering away out into ze blue,
Looking in vain for her lover,
He sailed in May '42.

So spare a kind thought for our feelings
As we struggle to maintain our light,
For we brighten somebody's darkness
Hunnishly yours – Conrad Veidt.

Alias Vic Jarvis,
Forest Hill.

Dear Terry,
This should be a letter to my solicitor, but you've put me off with that German's record; never mind about the human spray, can you

tell me what's wrong with the fair-haired lassie's eyes – is she blind or a bit of a simpleton – when with that lovely view across the bay she is standing at the door, freezing to her hair roots, staring at her stairs – or has she had my builders in?

Flo. Night-in-Gale,
Fishponds, Bristol.

Dear Terry Wogan,
With reference to your sarcastic comments about 'stairgazing', may I say that not only does such a thing go on, it is in fact a highly respectable and instructive pastime. Dear Conrad was one of the leading exponents of this craft in his time.
    I myself am secretary of the PESTS (Penrith Stairgazing Society) and we hold weekly sit-ins. Our motto is 'Well, I'll go to t'foot of our stairs' (said in a Derbyshire accent) and our aim is to promote true upward vision and to strengthen and respect all stairs and steps in the Penrith area. Our members sit on a different flight of stairs at each meeting and read extracts from our sacred writing. Such books as 'The Thirty Nine Steps' are held in special esteem.

Michael Ryan (PESTS),
Penrith, Cumbria.

N.B. Human spray, by the way, is used to clean stair carpets, hence its mention in our Lord Conrad's song.

As always, you had the hard-boiled cynic:

Sir,
Being an Estate Agent, I am well aware of the sneaking ways that some tenants have of voicing their grumbles, for instance, take this 'fair-haired lessee' who rents this cottage by the bay, she is obviously hoping that members of the local council will be listening to your programme, so that when she puts in for a rate reduction due to the excessive noise of the car breakers on the shore, she will receive sympathetic consideration.

Gerry Adams,
Pinner, Middlesex.

And the eejit who can never leave well enough alone:

***D**ear Terry,
As much as I like Conrad Veidt's rendering of the 'Lighthouse
across the Bay,' the original version had another verse which
appears to have been left out. Fortunately I can remember it, and
enclose the English and German words for your guidance.*

*Gladys,
Arrington.*

*Ich Kan nicht vergessen das nicht von denken
Sitzen alein nar der stinken und smellen
Wer essen der dunkencrunchen und Beer
Donner and blitzen! der aroma in mein ear!!
Das reinigen gross und fillen der Seine
Nicht vergessen dein bloomers
Bis du schane
Auf wiederschein meine liebling, auf
    wiederschein.*

*I cannot forget my last Evening with you
When we sat on the balcony next to the Loo
That memorable meal – pickled onions and beer
With the scent of your sweet breath as you nibbled
    my ear
The last ride on our Tandem, in spite of the rain
I remember your knickers got caught in the chain.
Goodbye My Love, Goodbye!*

Thanks to the public's amused interest the
record was re-issued as a single, and the bold Conrad Veidt
enjoyed a posthumous hit!
        All this talk of lighthouses opened a whole new
can of worms, when an eagle-eyed correspondent claimed to have
spotted another lighthouse! Nothing remarkable there, you cry.
Our island coastline is alive with the things. Too true, and I wasn't
inclined to put much pass on it myself, until the listener told me
where he'd spotted it: *Northampton!*
        I glossed over it, of course, merely remarking
that they were not all locked up yet , and returned to my real

morning's work of trying to eke a cup of coffee out of the BBC Canteen.

Next morning, I disappeared under a flood-tide of mail, all of it pointing out sharply that there *was* a lighthouse in Northampton, and I would do better not to scoff at things I didn't understand. Keith Pettit, village idiot of Moulton, enclosed a picture:

*D*ear Mr Wo be gon,
I have enclosed – as requested – a photo of the now famous Northampton Lighthouse. I do, of course, have a theory as to its use. I think the Government plans to reduce the unemployment figures – at a stroke – by submerging the whole of East Anglia, thus making Northampton a coastal town. This will of course be confirmed as soon as they start work on the pier.

Keith Pettit,
Moulton, Northampton.

P.S. We shall be open for Bed and Breakfast at very reasonable rates, come the big day.

Further confirmation came from Antigone Longhurst:

*D*ear Terence,
You and your correspondents are so IGNORANT. The structure being raised at Northampton IS a lighthouse. My husband and I, who carry marshmallows and thermal underwear between Leighton Buzzard and Wigan in our long-boat, will find it useful when it is complete.

Just south-west of Northampton we travel on the canal between Rothersthorpe and Gayton. We have, on almost every trip, collided into a nasty boulder on the west bank.

Please do not be so scathing of navigational aids.

Antigone Longhurst,
Marple, Cheshire.

I was still sceptical. (It takes a good one to get past me.) Notwithstanding the evidence, and the historical precedent of Wigan Pier, I couldn't see that a lighthouse 200 miles from the sea was going to do much good for Jolly Jack Tar on a gale-tossed ocean. Speculation was rife as to what the edifice might *really* be. A folly of some kind? A monument to Northampton grit and determination? A landmark for British Rail, who according to the locals keep missing Northampton? An inter-continental ballistic missile? Nikola Massingham had no doubt of its true purpose:

*D*ear Mr Wogan,
It is in fact a giant rhubarb cloche, you can see the first leaves sprouting through the top.

In early June, all the nation's gardeners will foregather in the Northampton Bus Station, a place of great beauty and grace. They will then march as one down the M1 to Westminster, carrying the giant rhubarb as a gesture of their feelings towards the 15% VAT on left-handed trowels.

Please do not reveal this information for fear of a custard attack as we pass through Watford. Perhaps YOU would be kind enough to lead the march, just in case the people of Watford do not put custard on their rhubarb.

Nikola Massingham,
Kislingbury, Northampton.

RIDICULOUS PLACE TO PUT A LIFT-TESTING TOWER!

Somebody had to spoil our little game in the end, of course. Express Lifts of Northampton claimed the thing was a lift-testing tower? I ask you, do these people take us for fools?

The road report

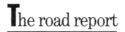

Apart from my cheery good-humour, nothing incenses the average listener more than the traffic reports from the BBC Motoring Unit. The good folk in the unit are sparing of neither nerve nor sinew, as they cull the news of the nation's roads from police forces up and down the country. However, it's easy to understand the frustration of a motorist trapped in the Blackwall Tunnel when he is informed that he ought to avoid it for the next two hours. Similarly, those watching their engines overheating as they sit motionless on the Chiswick Flyover are apt to grip the steering-wheel a little more tightly when told that the reason for a six-mile tail-back is a broken-down lorry, and that they should delay their journey into London or take another route. It's not much consolation, either, to be told that the Forth Road Bridge is now open again, and traffic is flowing freely in Fife....

Travelling as I do, sixty or so miles a day, mostly by motorway, in and out of London, I can readily identify with the traffic-snarled commuter. It can all get a bit tense and stressful, and I am ever seeking ways to enliven the be-jammed with jolly japes and wizard wheezes, suggesting that they smile vivaciously at the fuming driver in the adjoining lane, or blow kisses to that attractive lorry-driver throbbing beside you. I like to think that I have been instrumental in helping to start many a blossoming friendship. I may be wrong of course.

Bearing in mind the ever-increasing strain of driving on Britain's pock-marked motorways, it's refreshing to receive a letter like this, proving that the British motorist hasn't lost his sense of humour:

*D*ear *Terry.*

I am about to expose the mystery of the illuminated speed limit signs which most people think are there to warn of such things as fog or a nasty accident round the next bend. You may have wondered why the suggested speed limit never seems relevant to the road conditions but this is only because those of us who use the motorway system regularly are aware of the following code:

70 Out of order

50 This can have two meanings:
    a) beware of bright sunshine
    b) it was foggy here last week and although you can see clearly ahead for two miles the next sign like this is not until Carlisle and we are not taking any chances

30 We bet you wish you were able to do 30mph but until an hour ago the tail-back was not this far back

10 You have now been stationary for 15 minutes so please switch off your engine to conserve fuel. To avoid drowsiness try counting the number of little lights that make this sign work. The police car rushing backwards down the hard-shoulder with its lights flashing is distributing prizes to those with the correct answer.

Michael Pritchard,
Beaconsfield, Bucks.

The cones

Still on the vicissitudes of motorway driving, last year, in a recondite pensive moment, brought on, doubtless, by Manly Barrilow whining about something or other, I mentioned in passing how numerous the motorway 'cones' were becoming. It seemed extraordinary to me that although mile after mile of motorway lane was 'coned off', I never saw a soul working on the other side of the things. I may also have touched lightly on the nature of these little red and white excrescences, and perhaps even that such were their numbers they might well be breeding, since there appeared to be little or no supervision over them.

It was as if a veil had been lifted from the eyes of the British public. Suddenly, they began to see the supposedly innocuous 'cone' in its true light. Letters poured in, accompanied in many cases by photographs graphically depicting the dreaded cones about their evil work. Cones encircling a hole in the road, down which some unfortunate workmen had barely escaped with their lives; cones gathered round a telegraph pole, snapping at the heels of a terrified telephone engineer; cones hi-jacking lorries; cones intimidating police cars; cones blocking perfectly clear roads for their own fell purposes. It was clear that an epidemic was raging. Having insidiously wormed their way into the very fabric of British society, the little swine were beginning to flaunt their power openly! But where did they come from?

***D**ear Mr Wogan,*
ROAD CONES
It has been brought to my attention that on your radio programme you have recently been making disparaging comments about cones on the roads. I feel that I should point out that we at Edgeborough Farm are one of the largest growers of these cones. Each year we carefully cultivate the ground, sow seed and then meticulously, almost lovingly, tend the tender young growing cones. Now, just when we are about to harvest a bumper crop, your adverse comments threaten a disastrous slump in sales. This is particularly unfortunate at a time when we are facing increasing competition from French growers. Indeed, almost certainly we now face the prospect of a Common Market cone mountain. So come off it, Mr Wogan. Be fair to British cone growers.

Incidentally, your listener may have noticed that some cones are bigger than others and wondered what the difference is. To be honest, there is no difference. It's just that the

big ones have been growing longer. By careful and selective breeding, we have now produced a super cone. This grows at a truly alarming rate and reproduces itself so fast that even rabbits turn pale. Furthermore, this super cone shows an amusing tendency to devour any motorist who inadvertently hits it! Your listener is therefore advised to take care when passing these new cones.

G. D. Luff,
Edgeborough Farm, Guildford.

Shock Horror Probe!!! And then this:

Dear Terry,
It all started one dismal day on the M62, Conestance and Conerad were busy coneducting the traffic. One windy night the two were brought together and found themselves instantly attracted to each other. Conerad conefessed his love and the conesequence was they were married.

     The marriage drew cones from all over the conetry and they conegregated at Derby Works, Bury for the conetract of betrothal.

     The happy pair flew to Coney Island, USA on Conecorde for their honeymoon.

     Several months later they coneceived the little arrival in the parcel, they couldn't coneceal their joy, but it was short-lived. For a forty ton Pantechnicone lorry bowled Conestance and Conerad over on the A56 and their little orphaned baby Conenan was left alone in the world.

The Office,
Swintex Ltd,
Bury, Lancashire.

Panic set in. Wild-eyed people began to see cones everywhere. From T. V. Probert came these definitions:

> *Conequerors – the males of the species*
> *Conecubines – the females*
> *Conesummation – the mating season*
> *Conecoctions – the offspring*
> *Conetinents – the breeding grounds*
> *Chilli cone carne – what cones eat*
> *Conevore – predator of cones*
> *Boa Conestrictor – cone-eating snake*
> *Belisha Beacones – cones which glow at night*
> *Conequistadores – 'soldier' cones*
> *Icones – statues of cones on Greek motorways*
> *Cone-on-the-kerb – cones growing on the pavement*
> *Conestable – the law-enforcer*
> *Conetraband – illegal immigrants*

T. V. Probert,
Manchester.

I only hope they've got Mr Probert lying down in some darkened room somewhere. But worse was to come:

Dear Terry,

I have recently returned from the CONETINENT, where I attended a CONEFERENCE on CONECHOLOGY, which, as you will be aware, is the scientific study of CONEGESTION and CONEFUSION on the highways and by-ways of the developed countries. Many exciting and hitherto unpublished facts came to light. Cones have CONETRIBUTED many features of our own culture – CONEFETTI at weddings; CONESCRIPTION into the Armed Forces; the development of many of the world's best CONETRALTOS.

A word about their origins – they were invented close to my home in COLNE. Over the years, they have received such a battering from the travelling public that their name was shortened to CONE (they have had the 'ell knocked out of them).

Jim Ashton,
Nelson, Lancashire.

Then, as always, the Rebecca of Sunnybrook Farm spirit that is always bubbling merrily away 'neath the seething maelstrom of my daily mail-bag, began to burst through:

Dear Terry,

As cones seem to have become a part of everyday life these days, I thought that the education of our children would not be complete without the 'Children's Book of Cone Rhymes'. I enclose a selection from Volume 1 in the hope that you will rectify this gross negligence immediately.

Miss A. Mealing,
Penarth, S. Glamorgan.

> *Terry, Terry, quite contrary*
> *How do the motorways grow?*
> *With tarmac grey*
> *And men who play*
> *With pretty cones all in a row.*

Motorway policeman
Come blow on your horn,
The drivers are angry,
Their nerves frayed and torn.
The carriageway's blocked
With cone upon cone
But where are the workmen?
They've all gone home.

Oh where, oh where have the
workmen gone
Oh where, oh where can they be?
With a cone put here and a cone
put there
They must have gone to their tea.

Mister policeman have you any cones?
Yes sir, yes sir, for three zones.
One for the roadworks,
One for the mains
And one for the motorway to close up a lane.

I had a little cone tree
Nothing would it bear
But a silver fir cone
And a cone-shaped pear.
The King of Spain's daughter
Came to visit me
And all for the sake
Of my little cone tree.

Jack and Jill went up the hill
To fetch a pile of road cones
Jack fell down and broke a cone
And Jill was full of moans and groans.

Pat-a-cone, pat-a-cone motorway man
Close me a lane as fast as you can.
Stop it and block it, and mark it with glee
Put out your cones and go home to your tea.

This was smartly followed by a fairy-tale to uplift the most hardened of hearts:

Dear Mr Wogan,
My husband, who is a long-distance lorry driver, has asked me to write to you and tell you the true reason why there are so many cones on our highways and byways. You must have wondered why the weather is so bad this summer – well, the answer is in the cones.
The wicked bad-weather witch has turned all the sunshine fairies into cones. The men in red frocks are really the servants of the witch guarding the fairies. But all is not lost, there is a way to break every spell. Any lorry driver, as befits the knights of old, can save those fairies (and our summer) if he is bold and brave enough. All he has to do when he sees a little group of cones with their warder is to leap out of his cab and give the man in the red frock a great big kiss. All the cones will immediately turn back into sunshine fairies and we can all take our winter woollies off. Simple isn't it?

Ann Prior,
Exmouth, Devon.

After that what could one say? Well, Peter Isherwood said it for all of us:

Dear Terry Wogan,
Regarding all this hoo-ha about cones I can only say one thing –
Bollards!

Peter Isherwood,
Lytham St Anne's, Lancashire.

Coneclusion.

Twits (and other idiots)

First, there were the TWITS (Terry Wogan Is Tops Society), a devoted band of loonies who wear a T-shirt bearing their hero's facsimile and hold their annual general meeting in a phone-box just off Regent's Park. This proud and bonny band have their own hand-shake, sign and thing for taking the stones out of horses' hooves, but, of course, they could not expect to flourish alone. No sooner had the world heard of their inauguration, than every dog and devil was clambering aboard the bandwogan, and just as soon, jumping off again, preferably on good old Terence's neck:

Dear Terry,

I was led to believe that equal airspace was given to opposing parties. I therefore write to complain about the large amount of time allowed for the TWITS (Terry Wogan Is Tops) without even a single mention of the TWIST (Terry Wogan Is Singularly Tawdry) incorporating the TWIRL (Terry Wogan Is Really Lousy) and the TWINE (Terry Wogan Is Naturally Excruciating) parties.

I write to ask, nay demand, equal airtime for the ideals and policies of TWIST. If you do not succumb to our wishes we will have no option other than to pass this on to our debt collection agency.

Syd Balarsky,
Honorary Life President, TWIST,
Cambuslang, Lanarkshire.

I'M A MEMBER OF THE NATIONAL INSTITUTE OF TERRY WOGAN INSULTERS AND TAUNTERS

NITWIT

Nark it Syd, join the queue:

*D*ear Terry,
*I am a fully paid up member of WOGANS – Workshy, Overpaid,
Grousers and Naggers Society. . . .*

*Doris Tighe,
Warrington, Cheshire.*

Thank you, Doris, but in the matter of uncalled-for slurs, you're
only in the ha'penny place to this incognito:

*D*ear Mr Wogan,
*I can't think how you can stand there rabbitting on day after day
when the whole political future of our country is in the melting pot.
       I have heard that right-wing members of
TWADDLE (Terry Wogan And Daffy Duck Look Effeminate) are
to form a political alliance with EARWIG (Elderly Alcoholics
Reckon Wogan Is Gay) and sweep the board at the next general
election.
       One suggested name for the new party is WIDOW
(Wogan Is A Dreadful Old Woman). That should certainly unite
the voters!
       Just think, if you were to lead the new Party, you
could realise your great dream of appearing in a Party Political
Broadcast, and you could finish up as our first real woman Prime
Minister!*

*Anon,
N. Cornwall.*

*P.S. I hear you're leaving the BBC to start a banana farm in
Ireland. Here's a small contribution (½p) towards your fare. And
no backing out this time!*

I wouldn't mind, but manliness and cold showers
are watchwords on my programme. Thank heaven Louise Leed is
there to stand up for me:

In my capacity as a keen observer of rubbish on television, I watched aghast a thing called 'Hawaii'. I never quite grasped the gist of it, but a scene of singular horror that stuck in my memory was of Robert Wagner climbing from a swimming pool, the better to embrace Angie Dickinson. And who is there to blame him? The thing of singular horror, however, was Wagner's gut, which hung there, like some dozing leviathan, in the split second before he remembered to pull it in for the camera. I made some remark the following morning along the lines of a fellow-feeling we chubbies had felt, and stap the old vitals if I wasn't

immediately enrolled into ARMPITS: Association of Rotund
Males who Pull In Their Stomachs!

Then, on a Michael Parkinson show, the Seer of
Barnsley remarked that I appeared to have 'reached my peak'. I
demurred, coyly, on the grounds that peaks are as far as a body
can go, and indeed, there's only *one* way anybody can go *from* a
peak, and that's *down*. It stirred Pat Smith to write:

*D*ear Terry,
*Before you fall off your peak, which I hope you won't do for a few
days yet, here are a few slogans to keep you going:*

TWIRL - Terry Wogan Is Really Lovely

TWINE - Terry Wogan Is No Eejit

TWANG - Terry Wogan's A Nice Guy

TWILL - Terry Wogan - Ireland's Loveliest Lunatic

*TWIST - Terry Wogan Is So Tubby (I know how to wound don't I?
Never mind, I'm tubby too)*

TWERP - Terry Wogan's Excellent Radio Programme

TWINGE - Terry Wogan Is Not Getting Enough

TWEAK - Terry Wogan Expects A Knighthood

*Seriously though, I'm a great fan of yours and wish you many
more years at the peak.*

*Pat Smith (Mrs),
Cramlington, Northumberland.*

That'll be the day, although a discerning gobdaw recently
suggested that I already *was* an OBE (Overweight Babbling Eejit).

It's all just a little hurtful, but in moments of real
angst, when all fruit fails, there's always the IDIOTS. What!
You've never heard of the I Drool Incessantly Over Terry
Society?!?

Quick, nurse, the screens!

It's not a bit of use blaming me. He was here before I was (he was here before *everybody*) and yet *somebody* must have encouraged him, or how could he have lasted *this* long? And no, that's not my fault, either. He just appeared in my studio one morning at 9.40am, hunched up in his mobile commode, like the King of the Daleks, and I didn't have the heart to remove him.

Oh, I'm very well aware that I'll never get rid of him *now* – particularly after *The Gong*. Nurse wheels him in one morning, himself pleased as punch, wheezing away and pointing to a medal banging against his little chicken-chest. 'It's the OBE!' he cries, going into another paroxysm of coughing. 'Yes', I reply testily, 'Other Buggers' Efforts'. He doesn't like it, of course, but he's too excited to stop and consider, and rambles on, the veins in his legs throbbing dangerously. '*She* said she listens to our little chin-wag! What do you think about *that?*' I try and comfort him, because his little nose is turning puce. 'Very nice, you old fool – why didn't I get a gong then?' 'Har-har!' he chuckles, his apology for a chest heaving piteously with the effort. '*She* says it's the part of my programme she enjoys *best* – har-har-har!'

I could spit. Here he is, only surviving because of *my* kindness and generosity – only continuing to keep his old head out of the gas oven because I give him a couple of minutes on *my* programme and *She* thinks it's *his* programme. What the Sam Hill are Her advisers being paid for? By rights, that gong is *mine, mine,* do you hear?

Of course, as soon as there is mention of a decoration, you have the middle-class at your throat:

Sir,
I write at the request of my grandfather, Lt-Col (Rtd) Cuthbert Pukington-ssmyth, 44th Foot and Mouth (Submarine Lancers) to complain at the dastardly way you insult that fine upstanding British gentleman, James Young Esq.

He says, I quote: 'James Young did sterling work in the war, and us chaps home from the veldt on leave liked nothing better than to take a popsy to the old Alhambra in Leicester Square to see Mr Young perform. His renditions of 'The Boers Have Got

My Daddy' and 'Goodbye Dolly Gray' were first class and brought
tears to the eyes of even us chaps who are made of stern stuff.'

R. G. Castle,
Stevenage, Herts.

And the crawlers:

***D**ear Terry.*
Whoever it was, was right in saying the JY interlude is the best
part of your show; but then, it's also the best part of Jim's. A sort of
irresistible force meeting an immoveable object, though I wouldn't
hazard a guess as to which is which.

In the rarefied air of the BBC
Two minds magnificent meet and mingle;
And the brilliant flashes of repartee
Are sufficient to make one's toenails tingle.
The shafts of conversational wit,
The serendipitous well-turned phrase
Illumine the world of the listening twit,
And set his questioning mind ablaze.
Is someone wondering how to best
Distinguish these Lords of the wireless wave?
Well, Jimmy's the one with grubby vest,
And Terry's the one who needs a shave.

Joan Wells,
Benfleet, Essex.

Too right, Wells, particularly in the matter of the *vest.* I've never
seen it myself, mind. Its just a shadowy 'éminence grise', moving,
seemingly of its own volition, underneath the old artificer's drip-
dry crumpled polyester under-garment.

***D**ear Terry Wogan,*
We at TWANKY (Terry Wogan Association for Not Knocking
Youngs) would express our concern at your cruel baiting of plucky
Jim, the man who has brought the English language into the same
century as Australian cricket, French apples, and home-brewed

beer. The Youngs are good yeoman stock – remember Mighty Joe Young? Andrew Young? Egg Foo Young?

Brian Green,
Stevenage, Herts.

Any excuse for a bad joke, or three. Thank goodness there are members of the public not quite so easily gulled:

Dear Mr Wogan,
What a load of rubbish you and Jimmy Young talk about every morning! It reminds me of a nursery, Jimbo talks about things he knows nothing about, while you rabbit on about all the silly things that enter your head. I would make the pair of you redundant, and put Worzel Gummidge in charge, he couldn't do any worse than you two!

I will not remain anonymous,
I am Isaac Sibley of Leadgate,
Consett, Co. Durham.

Bless you for your forthrightness, old Isaac – and you, Miss Jan Swales of Sunny Skeggy:

Dear Terry,
Could you please tell me who is the poor old chap whom you are obliged to humour when he interrupts you each morning at 9.40? Is he perhaps your grand-daddy? I have been told that it's Jimmy Young, but I believe he died several years ago.

Jan Swales,
Skegness, Lincs.

Do you think I'd admit it, if he *was* my grand-daddy?
                    Then, friends, in a plain brown envelope, came
this heartening note:

OK Blue Eyes,
We have chosen your programme to reveal the latest step in our campaign – WE HAVE GOT JIMMY YOUNG. (Ingore pictures in

the dailies showing him leaving Heathrow airport for exotic climes with nubile young women – it's a stand-in, our special agent master-of-disguise, 'Fingers McCone'.) Disguise yourself as a brown paper parcel and meet our alluring conespirator Deirdre Bent at the Rat and Cockle, Hampstead, where our demands will be revealed. Be seein' ya.

Genny Reid,
Cones Popular Front,
Bedwas, Gwent.

I met Deirdre at the Rat and Cockle (and very nice too) and pressed armfuls of money on her – but she insisted on giving him back.

Still he's not that bad ... nobody could be *that* bad could they? No hard feelings, Jimbo, and here's a stave or two in praise of Queen Victoria's favourite broadcaster, from the rhyming traffic warden, Harry Hartill:

If you can sing a ballad
Tho' your chest is feeling sore,
If you can give an encore, when
No-one's asked for more.

If you can speak to Lords and
Kings, when other men have failed,
If you've got away with murder
Yet never have been jailed.

If you can make a midday meal
Out of an old fish bone
If you can cox the Oxford boat
And row it on your own.

If you can talk of 'Mins' and 'Progs'
And say 'TTFN'
Then you must be old Jimbo
Whose programme starts at ten.

Harry Hartill.

Have you seen this man?

One day at school Sarah (aged 9), of Solihull, was asked to write a description of 'Someone on Television'. Her teacher, Mrs. S. Shrimpton, sent in this:

Terry Wogan has black hair which is straight and greasy. His face is quite chubby and pink. He is always looking happy but sometimes disgusted at other peoples jokes. He is quite tall and well built and his suits are too small for him. He has got a deep voice and he has an Irish accent. Sometimes he puts on accents and they sound witty. He wears pink shirts and grey suits. His habits are, putting his hand under the back flap of his jacket and cocking his little finger up when he holds his lollypop microphone. He makes all of us laugh because he is amusing.

I am supposed to have no feelings, of course.